Handbook for K–8 Arts Integration

Handbook for K–8 Arts Integration

Purposeful Planning Across the Curriculum

Nan L. McDonald
San Diego State University

Boston • New York • San Francisco
Mexico City • Montreal • Toronto • London • Madrid • Munich • Paris
Hong Kong • Singapore • Tokyo • Cape Town • Sydney

Series Editor: Kelly Villella Canton
Series Editorial Assistant: Annalea Manalili
Vice President, Marketing and Sales Strategies: Emily Williams Knight
Vice President, Director of Marketing: Quinn Perkson
Senior Marketing Manager: Darcy Betts
Marketing Assistant: Robin Holtsberry
Production Editor: Cynthia Parsons
Editorial Production Service: Cynthia Parsons
Composition Buyer: Linda Cox
Manufacturing Manager: Megan Cochran
Electronic Composition: Omegatype Typography, Inc.
Interior Design: Omegatype Typography, Inc.
Cover Designer: Elena Sidorova

For related titles and support materials, visit our online catalog at www.pearsonhighered.com.

Between the time website information is gathered and then published, it is not unusual for some sites to have closed. Also, the transcription of URLs can result in typographical errors. The publisher would appreciate notification where these errors occur so that they may be corrected in subsequent editions.

Printed in the United States of America

Photo Credits

p. vi, Nan McDonald; p. 1, Khanh Pham; p. 11, Adrienne Laws; p. 27, Khanh Pham; p. 30, Rose Tanonis; p. 33, Adrienne Laws; p. 36, Kate Gray; p. 39, Khanh Pham; p. 41, Kate Crandall; p. 44, Christi Elmont; p. 47, Andy Soto; p. 57 Rose Tanonis; p. 75, Khanh Pham; p. 105, Khanh Pham; p. 117, Rose Tanonis; p. 118, Christi Elmont; p. 127, Kate Gray; p. 143, Colleen Crandall; p. 144, Kate Gray; p. 150, Colleen Crandall; p. 169, Rose Tanonis.

www.pearsonhighered.com

ISBN-10: 0-13-613813-6
ISBN-13: 978-0-13-613813-6

Dedication

In loving memory of Tom Lusk, stepfather and friend,
through whose generosity this book was written.

Nan L. McDonald, Ed.D., is Professor of Music at San Diego State University (SDSU) School of Music and Dance, where she teaches both future and practicing music and classroom teachers. Dr. McDonald has over 30 years of experience teaching music and integrated arts across the curriculum to K–8 students and teachers.

In 2003, Dr. McDonald received the SDSU Alumni Award for Outstanding Contributions to the University from the SDSU College of Professional Studies and Fine Arts. She has also been designated as the Outstanding Faculty Member in Liberal Studies (1999) and in the School of Music and Dance (2005), and as California Outstanding University Music Educator (2000) by the California Music Educators Association.

Dr. McDonald has authored and co-authored numerous scholarly publications. She is a National Program Author for Pearson Education/Silver Burdett Music *Making Music K–8* (2002, 2005) and *Making Music With the Arts Across the Curriculum* (2008). She and SDSU colleague Dr. Douglas Fisher have written two books for classroom teacher education, entitled *Teaching Literacy Through the Arts* (2006, Guilford) and *Developing Arts-Loving Readers* (2002, Rowman & Littlefield Education).

contents

chapter **1** *What Are the Arts, Their Standards,
and Their Impact on Student Learning?*   **1**

chapter 2 *What Students Need to Know*   27

chapter 5 *Instruction*   103

chapter 6 *Evaluation* **127**

chapter 7 *Unpacking the Arts Standards'
Big Ideas*   **151**

chapter 8 *Arts Within My Classroom and Beyond*   **169**

"Thumbnail Sketches": Additional Ideas from Our K–8 Contributing Classroom Teachers 178

Conclusion 186

References 186

APPENDIX: Resource Bibliography 187

Index 201

Across the nation, educators, parents, and others agree that young students need to learn about, create, do, and participate in the arts. While we know that all students (by law) deserve a complete education in the core content of the arts, that education is frequently marginalized and in some cases has been entirely eliminated from K–8 school curricula. Something else is needed to provide the arts to all students.

Many future and practicing classroom teachers seek to effectively teach *with* the arts (music, visual arts, theatre, and dance) *within and across* the K–8 content curriculum (i.e., math, science, social studies, language arts/literacy). However, there may be challenges to address. Once an integrated arts lesson model (read in a book, found on a website source, modeled by university methods teachers and master teachers, experienced in a professional growth workshop, etc.) has been replicated, some future and practicing teachers may wonder what to do next.

This book is designed to help future and practicing K–8 classroom teachers increase student understanding through purposefully planned arts infusion across the classroom curriculum. Specific purposes here are to teach K–8 standards-based classroom content and meet student needs through the inclusion of standards-based arts activities as a powerful way to teach, learn, do, know, and remember. Linked to this important purpose, this book is designed to increase both teachers' and their students' understanding and knowledge of the arts themselves.

You may or may not know how to plan standards-based, arts-infused lessons for your future or current students. However, if you and others can systematically develop and experiment with your own skills in purposefully planned teaching, assessments, and reflection you can begin to effectively use the arts more often and with increased confidence. You can also teach with increased purpose and creativity designed to maximize students' understanding of what they need to know across the content areas.

What Will I Get From This Book?
What Is Purposeful Planning With the Arts?

This book establishes a constructive and reflective process (purposeful planning) designed to help teachers facilitate K–8 student understanding through arts-activity infusion across the curriculum. Throughout the book, you will consider effective ways to use the arts across the standards-based classroom curriculum. This book guides you to *construct* your own ability to plan, teach, and evaluate your own art-infused lessons linked to what your future or current students need to know within other content areas.

You and your university methods class peers (in teaching labs) or your current K–8 students will learn more about the arts, their content standards, teaching, and assessment through the various planning and evaluation activities you will complete both individually and with others.

K–8 Contributing Teachers:
Connections to Classroom Realities

Several practicing K–8 classroom teachers have participated in the same planning processes and considerations you will address throughout this book. These contributing teachers have provided many real-life classroom vignettes related to each of the planning stages you will read about and engage in (chapter by chapter) throughout the book. Through their creative descriptions and reflections, you will be provided realistic food for thought along with debriefing interviews, analysis, and discussion of their ideas and experiences.

"Lesson Tracker" Boxes

As you read our contributing teachers' many classroom vignettes, an accompanying text box, "Lesson Tracker," will guide you through the following key information (each "Lesson Tracker" will be matched to information pertinent to that particular chapter's focus):

- "Big ideas" addressed within the lesson: "What students need to know"
- Content standards involved (for arts and across the curriculum content areas)
- Considerations/steps in planning
- Materials list
- Teaching strategies and sequence
- Assessments and evaluation techniques

How Do I Use This Book?

Remember that this book is designed to help you plan and implement successful arts-infused activities across the classroom curriculum. As such, the book is *both* a self-study and a group interactive experience (to be used in methods classes and/or with practicing teacher peers on-site).

For these reasons, the book and accompanying self-study exercises and discussions are meant to be read and completed sequentially, chapter by chapter, to build or construct your knowledge about and success and comfort with using arts activities in everyday teaching.

Each chapter will feature some or all of the following additional features:

- *Focus Activity:* Anticipatory ("agree or disagree") survey to use before and after reading the chapter and for group discussions. There is also an Attitude Survey following this Introduction, to be filled in before and then after reading this book.
- *Musings:* Chapter opening quotes from a variety of sources—artists, teachers, philosophers, curriculum experts, poets, etc.—related to the chapter content that follows that quote or idea.
- *In the Classroom:* Direct, detailed vignettes from contributing teachers' (K–8) lessons across the curriculum.
- *Lesson Tracker:* A series of inserts outlining or tracking the key features of a particular "In the Classroom" lesson example.
- *Teacher Debriefing* and *Reflections:* Analytical interviews with a K–8 contributing teacher about the "why, how, what, and what happened" in their "In the Classroom" example.
- *Discussion:* Analytical discussion of key features of a teacher-contributor's lesson, planning, or evaluation processes.
- *Beyond the Classroom:* Ideas and resources for extending important learning in the arts beyond the school environment, including the following: websites, arts providers and organizations, museums, community activities, home, family, and neighborhood interactions, and other people, places, and things.
- *Side-bar snippets:* Margin notes with resources, techniques, ideas, websites, and other "food for thought" information adding to your understanding of the text focus at hand.
- *Self-Study exercises:* End-of-chapter forms and suggestions for individual planning processes and peer discussions. Through these self-study exercises you will be guided (chapter by chapter) to create, plan, teach, and evaluate your own arts-infused lesson idea(s). You will construct a "personalized file" of lesson ideas (your own and those shared by methods class or school-site peers).
- *Appendix: Resource Bibliography:* This materials and resource list is provided at the end of the book. You will have the opportunity to search for and evaluate many additional websites, books, and other materials related to arts-infused lessons across the K–8 curriculum.

- *Customized arts-infused lesson file:* Suggestions will be made for you to create and share a customized file of integrated lessons for your future or current classroom and/or grade level. Forms will be provided within this book's text. These may be photocopied or adapted for online use and exchange among methods class and school-site peers.

Finally, throughout this book, you will be constantly considering "doable", everyday ways to creatively and effectively use arts activities linked to your own curriculum needs, comfort levels, and the needs of your students. Rather than seeking to merely duplicate prescribed lesson formulas, rules, or "recipes" toward arts integration, you will be empowered to think of your *own* ideas. You will have opportunities to develop ideas to teach and reflect on in your own methods class teaching labs or in your on-site teaching. By doing so, you will be able to create and share a customized "file" of arts-infused lessons with peers.

a c k n o w l e d g m e n t s

This book could not have been possible without the mentoring of my longtime colleague and collaborator, Dr. Douglas Fisher, San Diego State University. His belief in me and advocacy for arts within the curriculum have been a sustaining force in my professional life.

A team of devoted K–8 inner-city classroom teachers trusted me to deliver their messages about teaching with and through the arts across the curriculum. This book literally vibrates with the reality of their (and their young students') creativity and energy. Rose Tanonis, Adrienne Laws, Kate Gray, Khanh Pham, Colleen Crandall, Andy Soto, and Christi Elemont of the City Heights Educational Collaborative (Rosa Parks Elementary School and Monroe-Clark Middle School, San Diego Unified School District), you are my heroes and have taught me much.

Special thanks for the encouragement and understanding of friends Susan Greene, Pearson/Silver Burdett Music; Dr. Terry O'Donnell, San Diego State University; Miles Moore, Advanced Warning Systems; and Kathy Jones, San Diego State University Instructional Technology Services during the writing of this book. You gave me courage to complete this project through some very difficult times.

I would like to acknowledge the following reviewers who offered their thoughtful comments and suggestions as the work progressed: Denise A. Collins, The University of Texas at Arlington; Gayla C. Foster, Oklahoma State University; Nancy Johnson, Geneva College; Ana Marie Klein, SUNY Fredonia; Sandi MacLeod, University of Vermont; Wendy McLeish, Buffalo State College; Lisa N. Mitchell, Appalachian State University; Jody R. Paulson, University of Montana; Nancy S. Self, Texas A&M University; Donna Thompson, San Jose State University; David E. Walker, Bloomsburg University of Pennsylvania. Through this important feedback, the book improved and evolved. And finally, former editor Meredith Fossel and current editor Kelly Villella Canton provided me support from concept through production. To them, I am especially grateful.

The following survey may be completed (both *before* and then *after* reading this book) to assess your attitudes, opinions, background knowledge and experiences, needs, and concerns regarding planning and teaching with the arts across the classroom curriculum.

Attitude Survey

Directions: Fill out this survey both before AND after reading this book. Place a 1–5 (see below) rating next to each statement in the appropriate column.

5 = Strongly Agree
4 = Agree
3 = Neither Agree or Disagree
2 = Disagree
1 = Strongly disagree

Before reading 1–5 rating		After reading 1–5 rating
	1. The arts should be taught by arts specialists (music, dance, theatre, visual art) only.	
	2. Students can increase understanding through arts activity connected to other content area instructional goals.	
	3. I am comfortable with the idea of using the arts in connection with other learning across my classroom curriculum.	
	4. I am concerned that I am not artistically talented and it will adversely affect my planning for arts-infused lessons.	
	5. I am able to imagine what arts activities I would use in arts-infused lessons across the curriculum.	
	6. "Knowledge" is "understanding."	
	7. I can imagine ways in which arts activities could help fill the gap between what students already know and what they need to know about a chosen topic.	

	8. One or more of the arts are within my "comfort zone" for teaching.	
	9. I do not have time or expertise to look for arts-infused lesson materials	
	10. Resources need to show me *how* to use those arts materials in a prescribed teaching sequence.	
	11. I have had some positive experiences teaching arts activities.	
	12. I know of or have a set of procedures and techniques to teach with each of the arts.	
	13. I am comfortable experimenting with a variety of ways to teach with the arts across the curriculum.	
	14. I have/know a set of procedures and techniques to assess and evaluate arts-infused learning activities and student end products.	
	15. I am able to access and use state and/or district arts content standards in Music, Dance, Theatre, and Visual Art.	
	16. I know ways to plan, teach, and assess arts standards within arts-infused lessons across the curriculum.	
	17. Much of the language within the arts content standards seems exclusively aimed at arts specialists and is *not* appropriate for classroom teacher use.	
	18. I would like to create and share a customized lesson file of arts-infused lesson ideas.	
	19. School site administration, district leadership, and parents will be supportive of arts-infused lessons across the curriculum.	
	20. My surrounding community offers many resources for use in arts-infused teaching. I am able to locate and use those resources.	
Point total BEFORE: _____	**Amount of CHANGE in point totals, if any** *(subtract "before" column from "after" column):* _____	**Point total AFTER:** _____

Handbook for K–8 Arts Integration

chapter 1

What Are the Arts, Their Standards, and Their Impact on Student Learning?

In my classroom, the arts bring voice and life to students' thoughts, emotions, and connections to their learning. This learning engages them in a multi-sensory way. It is a safe haven for expression.

—Carlie Ward, grade 5 teacher

FOCUS ACTIVITY

Directions: Please fill out before and after reading this chapter.

Before Reading Chapter A = agree D = disagree	Statements	After Reading Chapter A = agree D = disagree
	The arts (Music, Visual Art, Theatre, and Dance) are core content areas.	
	The arts should be taught by arts specialists (music, dance, theatre, visual art) only.	
	There are arts specialists at (my or local) K–8 school site(s).	
	Classroom teachers should use arts activity within other content area instruction.	
	Students can increase understanding through arts activity connected to other content area instructional goals.	
	I am comfortable with the idea of using the arts in connection with other learning across my classroom curriculum.	

Welcome. By answering the Focus Activity questions, you have already begun an interesting and constructive inquiry. One goal of this book is to guide you through an individual process to purposefully plan, teach (at school sites or lab groups within methods classes), and evaluate customized standards-based arts activity within K–8 content area instruction.

This first chapter offers information about the arts, their content standards, and the impact of arts activity on student learning and achievement. After this discussion, you will read two stories of real K–8 classroom teachers engaged in purposeful planning, teaching, and evaluative processes. These two vignettes describe how and why arts activities (music, visual art, theatre, and dance) were utilized to increase student interest, participation, and memory of specific learning tied to other content area instructional goals.

What Are the Arts?

Arts as Core Content

The arts are, by law, core content containing *four* distinct disciplines (music, visual arts, theatre, and dance) and are therefore worthy of study unto themselves.

National education goals were announced in 1990 and "with the passage of the *Goals 2000: Educate America Act*, the national goals are written into law naming the arts as a *core academic subject*—as important to education as English, mathematics, history, civics and government, geography, science and foreign language" (Consortium of National Arts Education Associations, 1994, p. 131). As such, *all* students by law deserve and should have access to specialized instruction (an education in the arts) taught by specialists in all four arts disciplines.

Who Will Teach the Arts?

As you know, the Arts (composite word for all four arts disciplines) may not be afforded the same consideration for instruction (teacher preparation courses, district funding, school scheduling, specialized arts teachers, facilities, materials, curriculum development, professional growth, etc.) as the other core content areas of language arts, mathematics, science, and social studies. (Physical education may also be marginalized.)

Core curriculum in all four arts is frequently not available or is delivered in a marginalized, nonsupported manner to school children (Leonhard, 1991; Stake, Bresler & Mabry, 1991; McDonald & Fisher, 2002, 2006). *Specialized* instruction for *all* students in each of the four arts (taught by teachers with specialized degrees and credentials in those specific arts) may not be available at most K–8 school sites. In other words, although the four arts are core academic content, the delivery of a specialized education in all four arts for every child is at best, challenged, and many times, totally unavailable.

The reality at many schools is that specialized education in the arts is limited to music or music and visual art. Furthermore, *many K–8 schools do not have arts specialists*, and the responsibility to include core content in the arts may rest with classroom teachers, falling under the nonspecialist instructional umbrella of arts within general education. With these situations in mind, how can the arts be made available to as many students as possible within general education contexts (nonspecialized arts instruction) taught by classroom teachers?

Classroom Teachers: General Education
With and Through the Arts

In order to deliver arts instruction to as many students as possible, the inclusion of arts activities within general curriculum instruction is becoming an important focus for future and practicing classroom teachers. Classroom teachers can and do successfully infuse customized arts activities within and tied to other content area standards-based instructional goals (e.g., purposeful musical activity within a standards-based, thematic social studies/history lesson; art illustration tied to specific language arts (literacy) lesson goals; theatre (reader's theatre) activity designed around factual "big ideas" in a lesson about the night sky; etc.) (McDonald & Fisher, 2006).

Furthermore, many educators also believe that young students need *both* specialized arts education and frequent learning opportunities that regularly *infuse* arts activity into everyday general classroom instruction as a powerful way of teaching, learning, doing, knowing, and connecting learning across the curriculum (Barrett, 2001; Barrett, McCoy & Veblen 1997; Barry, 1998; Cornett, 2006; Gelineau, 2003; Hancock, 2007; McDonald, 2008; McDonald & Fisher, 2002, 2006; Snyder, 2001). In the best of these learning contexts, standards-based arts activity is successfully paired with other content and student learning needs across the curriculum thereby increasing student understanding of the learning at hand. This takes careful, *purposeful planning*.

What Is Purposeful Planning With and Through the Arts?

Purposeful planning with and through the arts is a reoccurring theme and an ongoing, individualized self-study process you will follow throughout this book. This process includes your review of what young students already know and need to know within grade-level, standards-based, content area instruction. Purposeful planning requires the teacher to define and focus on the "big ideas" that need to be taught, learned, and remembered by students.

Appropriate standards-based arts activities are then developed and infused into other content instruction with the purpose of increased student participation, learning, understanding, and memory of the learning at hand. Importantly, this learning includes increasing student and classroom teacher's knowledge of the arts themselves.

Appropriate, useable, and doable arts-infusion materials and resources must be located, created, or developed. Opportunities are designed by the teacher for young students to do, make, create, perform, display, analyze, review, and reflect upon their arts-infused lessons and learning across the curriculum. Throughout these processes, teachers and students are encouraged to reflect upon their experiences and tie them to content learning at hand.

Arts-infused lessons are easily assessed and evaluated by the teacher and young students to determine if content learning goals were accomplished (achievement) and how and why (and to what extent) the arts experiences impacted that teaching and learning. Finally, in purposeful planning, classroom teachers develop ways of constructing, using, evaluating, and sharing with peers a customized file of arts-infused lessons across their curriculum.

In order to successfully infuse and connect arts activities within other content area instruction, future and practicing classroom teachers must first become familiar with the arts content standards as they begin their purposeful planning processes. It's time to review those standards now.

Standards in the Arts

The national standards in the Arts (on which all state and district arts standards are based) were written for arts specialists and intended for use within specialized arts instruction. Yet, it is helpful to read and review these standards (see Table 1.1, "Arts Content Standards," p. 6) as you begin to make translations and applications toward your own future or current classroom teaching. Information offered in the Focus Activity may also help you begin to consider what elements, concepts, and activities within each of the four arts content standards are most *appropriate* for your own use, understanding, abilities, background, and current comfort level in the arts.

Suggestions for Standards-Based Arts Activities

As you make your way through this book's many K–8 classroom vignettes and your own upcoming planning processes, the information in Table 1.2, "Activities Students Can Do in the Four Arts," (p. 7) may be of help to you. This list was created by classroom teachers and offers some initial suggestions for standards-based, hands-on concepts and activities in each of the four arts. In it you may find ideas and activities that may be appropriate for your future or current teaching in the K–8 general classroom.

1.1 Understanding the Art Standards

As you read the following preliminary information based on the national standards in all four arts, note that a more comprehensive look at specific, discipline-based, arts content standards is offered in Chapter 7 of this book. As you read this book chapter by chapter, you will naturally become more familiar with arts standards and real-life classroom applications through teacher vignettes and accompanying "Lesson Tracker" analyses offered throughout. You will also use your own state's arts content standards as you complete the sequenced planning phases within self-study activities at the end of several chapters of this book.

1.2 Research your own state and district arts content standards.

Go online to your state's Department of Education and/or your local school district(s) and look for content or instructional standards in the Visual and Performing Arts (VAPA). There you may find standards listed by individual arts discipline (music, visual art, theatre, and dance) and grouped by sequenced grade-level expectations. Locate the grade level you teach or wish to teach. Keep these standards handy as you read this book and complete the sequenced self-study exercises at the end of several chapters.

Table 1.1 Arts Content Standards

National Music Content Standards include:
1. Singing, alone and with others, a varied repertoire of music
2. Performing on instruments, alone and with others, a varied repertoire of music
3. Improvising melodies, variations, and accompaniments
4. Composing and arranging music within specified guidelines
5. Reading and notating music
6. Listening to, analyzing, and describing music
7. Evaluating music and music performances
8. Understanding relationships among music, the other arts, and disciplines outside the arts
9. Understanding music in relation to history and culture

National Visual Arts Content Standards include:
1. Understanding and applying media, techniques, and processes
2. Using knowledge of structures and functions
3. Choosing and evaluating a range of subject matter, symbols, and ideas
4. Understanding the visual arts in relation to history and cultures
5. Reflecting on and assessing the characteristics and merits of their work and the work of others
6. Making connections between visual arts and other disciplines

National Theatre Content Standards include:
1. Script writing by planning and recording improvisations based on personal experience and heritage, imagination, literature, and history
2. Acting by assuming roles and interacting in improvisations
3. Designing by visualizing and arranging environments for classroom dramatizations
4. Directing by planning classroom dramatizations
5. Researching by finding information to support classroom dramatizations
6. Comparing and connecting art forms by describing theatre, dramatic media (such as film, television, and electronic media), and other forms
7. Analyzing and explaining personal preferences and constructing meanings from classroom dramatizations and from theatre, film, television, and electronic media productions
8. Understanding context by recognizing the role of theatre, film, television, and electronic media in daily life

National Dance Content Standards include:
1. Identifying and demonstrating movement elements and skills in performing dance
2. Understanding choreographic principles, processes, and structures
3. Understanding dance as a way to create and communicate meaning
4. Applying and demonstrating critical and creative thinking skills in dance
5. Demonstrating and understanding dance in various cultures and historical periods
6. Making connections between dance and healthful living
7. Making connections between dance and other disciplines

Source: MENC, 1994, pp. 23–72.

Table 1.2 Activities Students Can Do in the Four Arts

Theatre	Art	Music	Dance
reader's theatre	found art	songs	movement response
role playing	painting	instruments	pantomime
pantomime	sketching	chants/raps	movement to poetry
puppets	crayons	listening to music	movement to ideas
masks and characters	papier mâché	poetry and music	keeping a beat
script writing	clay/sculpture	rhythmic response	movement to words
finger plays	scratch art	found instruments	games
action to words	photography	composing	moving with props
scenery design	textiles	history of music	nonverbal communication
lighting design	artist study	compose song lyrics	body percussion
sets and costumes	torn paper art	music of the world	dances of the world
tableaux of scenes	mosaics	symbols of music	dances of different eras
creative drama games	pastels/chalk	reading music	popular dances
	charcoal	study composers	created dances
	water color	styles of music	gestures—no words
	pottery	science of sound	movement tableaux
	crafts	environmental sounds	
	jewelry	sound effects	
	tie-dye	music and mood	
	print making	musical theatre	
	stamp art	performing music	
	vegetable stamps	write about music	
	murals	write about musicians	
	stencil art		
	fashion		
	history of art		
	art of many cultures		
	computer art		
	write about art		
	study artist styles, lives		
	science of color		
	dioramas		

Note: This list was created by a group of 35 K–8 classroom teachers.

Source: From *Teaching Literacy Through the Arts* (p. 3), by N. L. McDonald and D. Fisher, 2006, New York: Guilford. Reprinted with permission.

It might be pertinent now to consider some more information concerning *why* teachers should teach with the arts within the general curriculum and the effect of those learning experiences on student achievement.

Recent academic research about the effect of the arts on learning has been compiled into a pivotal study, *Critical Links: Learning in the Arts and Student Academic and Social Development* (Arts Education Partnership, 2002). (Note: For a complete listing of specific research studies, refer to the complete version of "Critical Links" available online at www.aeparts.org/cllinkspage.htm. Reference the specific art to locate supporting studies connected to learning in other content areas.)

Research on the Impact of Arts Activity on Student Learning

Why Use the Arts Within Content Area Instruction?

The arts are important, but why should you take the time to develop yet another instructional consideration to incorporate across your future or present classroom curriculum? The answers are many. The arts make all kinds of learning exciting. The more involved students are, the more they learn and remember. The "making and doing" in arts activities can also

uniquely stimulate the senses and provide direct, active pathways to perceptions about the world around us. The arts provide a wealth of experience related to forms of human expression found in language as well as various forms of nonverbal and sensory communications such as gesture, emotions, feelings, sound, symbols, movement, shapes, colors, patterns, and designs (Gardner, 1984, 1993a, 1993b). Dance, theatre, music, and the visual arts often communicate within nonverbal avenues of expression and use symbols that are simply not translatable to human language. By doing so, they provide important ways of knowing as essential forms of human discourse and inquiry (Eisner, 1980). Human language alone may not provide the sufficient means to communicate many life experiences, emotions and meanings (California Department of Education, 1996). (within McDonald & Fisher, 2002, p. 4)

How Does Participation in Arts Activities Impact Student Achievement and Learning?

Figure 1.1, "How Students Benefit From Activity in the Arts" provides some further, in-depth reasons to include the arts within and across the K–8 general curriculum.

Learning Through the Arts: Student Academic and Social Development

According to a summary essay by James S. Catterall, "The Arts and the Transfer of Learning" (located within the larger comprehensive compilation of recent research studies, *Critical Links: Learning in the Arts and Student Academic and Social Development*, by Arts Education Partnership, 2002), student learning is positively impacted by arts activities in the following areas:

FIGURE 1.1   How Students Benefit From Activity in the Arts

- **Students learn through activities in the arts** by utilizing systems that include students' "integrated sensory, attentional, cognitive, emotional, and motor capacities and are, in fact, the driving forces behind all other learning" (Jensen, 2005, p. 2).
- **Students can benefit from activity in the arts,** "including students who are marginalized or underserved, at-risk, and those children with special needs. Students who receive learning opportunities with the arts benefit from better communication skills, friendships with others, and fewer instances of violence, racism, and other troubling and nonproductive behaviors (Fiske, 1999)."
- **Engagement in arts activities can increase important literacy skills** because students read, write, speak, and listen as they participate in the arts, and the arts themselves encourage new types of literacy to emerge (Armstrong, 2003).
- **K–8 students learn though doing, creating, making art, and participating in arts-related activities, performances, and displays.** Engagement and attention are key to learning (Marzano, 2004). "Hands-on and minds-on activities with and through the arts allow students explore content in new ways" (McDonald & Fisher, 2006, p. 6).
- **Students need to connect and exercise what they have learned throughout their school day.** Students learn within and across many contexts. Rather than thinking of math, science, social studies, or literacy/language arts as "something we've got to do every morning or afternoon," we want students to use what they have learned *throughout* the school day. The arts can help provide those contexts for connections. For instance, if you begin to use arts activity to increase student's literacy skills, you can also naturally design opportunities for students to connect this learning to social studies, math, and science (Jacobs, 1989, 1997).
- **When students participate in arts activities, their learning can provide them with needed cultural relevance** "through connections to various cultures, times, and their unique contribution of visual art, music, theatre, and dance" (McDonald & Fisher, 2006, p. 6).
- **Through the arts, students can enhance their creativity and increase satisfaction and involvement with the learning at hand.** "Classroom teachers consistently report that they and their students are happiest and most productive when engaged in creative ways of learning the arts naturally provide. Many teachers also report that these are the most meaningful and memorable learning experiences for their students" (McDonald & Fisher, 2006, p. 6).

Learning through Musical Activity: cognitive development, spatial reasoning, quality and prolixity of writing, mathematics proficiency, self-efficacy and concept, reading and SAT verbal scores, English skills of ESL learners

Learning through Visual Art Activity: content and organization of writing, reading skills and interpretation of text, reasoning about scientific images, reading readiness

Learning through Theatre/Drama: story comprehension (oral and written), character identification and motivation, amount of peer interaction, writing proficiency and prolixity, conflict resolution skills, focused thinking, understanding of social relationships and emotions, engagement and involvement, skills applied to new texts, problem-solving, self-concept

Learning through Dance/Movement: self-confidence, persistence, reading skills, nonverbal reasoning, expressive skills, creativity in poetry, social tolerance, group and individual social development

Learning through Integrated Arts Activities within Content Area Instruction positively impacts student learning and instructional environments in the following areas: leadership, reading, verbal, and mathematics skills; creative thinking; achievement; motivation; cognitive engagement; instructional practice in the school; professional culture of the school; school climate; and community engagement and identity

Learning through Arts-Rich School Environments is linked to the following: creativity, engagement/attendance, range of personal and social developments, and higher order thinking skills

Arts Infusion in Action: Classroom Vignettes

You may now wish to consider direct applications to the realities of K–8 classroom instruction. As you read the following classroom teacher vignette, keep in mind two important questions:

1. How do these two classroom teachers teach with the arts in a nonspecialized manner (arts within the general curriculum)?
2. Specifically, how do these teachers understand, address, communicate, and assess the arts and other content area standards; effectively plan for what students need to know; seek and find materials; use best practices in teaching; and evaluate their lessons connected to specific standards-based learning goals across content areas?

● IN THE CLASSROOM

Integrating Language Arts/Literacy with the Arts: "Orchid Paragraphs" Content Areas: Literacy/Language Arts, Arts (Visual Art, Music)

My students are all second language learners and have trouble speaking and writing in English. I decided to give them a language experience lesson so they would all have something to write about, little did I know to what level the students would take this.

—Adrienne Laws, second-grade teacher

Observation: **Mrs. Laws** guides me over to the class bulletin board display area. There, I see her inner-city second-grade students' beautiful still-life illustrations (crayon, pastel, and charcoal renditions) of a flower (orchid) paired with samples of their descriptive paragraphs. I asked Mrs. Laws about the lesson.

During this "Orchid Paragraphs" set of lessons, Mrs. Laws invited an artist relative to teach her children how to view a flower still life, create original art, and write about what they saw and illustrated. Later the same week, Mrs. Laws helped students to read books about painters and their craft and guided them to websites and library books about painting and painters as well as other activities based on this active arts experience and connected to goals within her writing instruction.

Mrs. Laws exclaimed, "Can you believe the writing that came out of this experience?" A student added, "Look over there, that one's mine!"

1.4 Content Standards Reminder

Remember that the language of the all content area instructional standards varies greatly from state to state, district to district. In order to meet this challenge, every effort has been made to use generalized terms to describe various content area standards within the lessons in this book. Although the standards used here are based on the California Content Standards used by our teacher contributors, it is hoped that translations and applications to your own state content standards can be easily made.

"Mr. Marcell taught us how to make art with a real model. He showed us orchid flowers and how to draw them. First, wee drew a box, then one long stem. Next, we drew some leaves and dirt in the box. Last, we drew the flower. Mr. Marcell also taught us about blending colors, 3-dimensional objects, even shading also he taught us about pollen. We learned about an artist's signature and about an artist's perspective. He told us that the stem holds the flower and can also provide depth in our live model. Mr. Marcell is Mrs. Laws' father."
By Dinh Chau

Mrs. Laws's "Orchid Paragraphs" lesson: Sample of student artwork and writing by second-grade student Dinh Chau.

Photo by Adrienne Laws.

One student sample read:

Mr. Marcell taught us how to make art with a real live model. He showed us orchid flowers and how to draw them. First we drew a box, and then one long stem. Next we drew some leaves and dirt in the box. Last we drew the flower. Mr. Marcell also taught us about blending colors, three-dimensional objects, even shading, also he taught us about pollen. We learned about an artist's signature and an artist perspective. He told us that the stem holds the flower and can provide depth in our live model. Mr. Marcell is Mrs. Laws's father. By Dinh Chau

• l e s s o n   t r a c k e r

Mrs. Laws's "Orchid Paragraphs"

- **Big Ideas:** Students need to develop and use new vocabulary in writing (brief narratives) and speaking based on direct experience in visual arts. Visual arts activity can generate new vocabulary and interest in writing and speaking about that hands-on activity.

- **Content Standards Addressed**

  Grade 2: Language Arts (Writing)—Write brief narratives based on experience, report on a topic with supportive facts and details, listen and speak (oral communication), recount experiences in a logical sequence.

  Grade 2: Visual Arts—Develop perceptual skills and Visual Arts vocabulary (balance, mood, warm and cool colors); analyze art elements and principles of design (line, color, shape/form, texture, and space); create original work of art (drawing, pastels); use this vocabulary in writing and speaking about an artist's demonstration and one's own individual work of art.

Teacher Debriefing: Mrs. Laws's Grade 2 Art and Literacy Lesson

Big ideas tied to content standards

Q: How and why did you (Mrs. Laws) choose your integrated instructional theme?

Mrs. Laws: My students are all second language learners and have trouble speaking and writing in English. I decided to give them a language experience lesson so they would all have something to write about. Little did I know to what level the students would take this. They wanted to check out art books and books about artists from the library. They wanted to use every new vocabulary word they learned in their writing.

Q: Why did you choose to integrate visual art activity into your classroom literacy instruction?

Mrs. Laws: I have found that art and music are a universal language for children and can lead to richer learning experiences. Many of my students are tactile and visual learners so I anticipated this was something they would enjoy.

Q: What were your standards-based, "big ideas" literacy goals for this lesson unit?

Mrs. Laws: I wanted my second graders to write brief narratives based on *direct* experiences. First of all, they needed a *real* reason to write, based on what they learned and enjoyed. They needed to think about what they did in the art activity and organize ideas for their descriptive paragraphs. I wanted my students to improve their ability to sequence their descriptions and incorporate detail and new vocabulary into their writing. I wanted to connect to visual art to have hands-on experiences with concepts and new vocabulary of space, shading, warm and cool colors, lines, artist perspective, etc., and ask students to use that new vocabulary about visual art in their writing. They also needed to discuss and edit their writing with others and make revisions for their final paragraphs.

l e s s o n   t r a c k e r

Mrs. Laws's "Orchid Paragraphs"

Considerations/Steps in Planning

- English language learners are tactile learners and need a reason to write based on real experiences.
- ELLs (English language learners from several language bases in this classroom) need a visual arts experience (e.g., a visiting artist and hands-on project) to develop perception and active use of art vocabulary in speaking and writing. *Visual Art teaching/learning accommodations were made (observation/direct drawing) to help overcome language barriers (student comprehension/fluency) during verbal instruction and demonstrations.*
- Students need to think about what they did in the art experience and sequence descriptions and new vocabulary into writing.
- Students need to discuss, edit, and revise their own writing with others.

Teaching strategies/sequences

Q: What happened during the lesson?

Mrs. Laws: The students were heterogeneously grouped with five students in a group, and they were rotated into my father's group every 35 minutes. He did a quick sketch to demonstrate technique introducing new vocabulary as he drew. The students were so excited and were impressed by his talents that you could only hear "ooh's" and "aah's" as he demonstrated. Then he distributed materials and took students step by step, sketching out their still life using pencils and using the new art terms. [Mrs. Laws and her guest used accommodations in visual art teaching techniques to help her English language and special learners in oral comprehension and vocabulary during initial modeling and instruction. These students were from several native language bases other than English. According to Mrs. Laws, "only one student knew what an orchid was." She determined her students needed to follow the artist in a nonverbal way and then apply English language terminology during and after their hands-on experiences (observation/drawing practice). They then went on to create their own unique interpretations of an orchid still life.]

Then he showed them how to add color, shading, and draw a table line so their artwork wasn't floating in the air. Then they verbally recounted their steps and what they learned before the next group rotated in.

The following day we made a web with the new art terms we learned and in pairs orally recounted what we learned. Then each student was to write a paragraph about his/her experience, have two friends edit his/her work before showing it to me. We conferred during writer's workshop and then the students did a good copy, which was put up under their art work, and a copy of their work was sent to my father, who in return wrote the class about their writing.

lesson tracker

Mrs. Laws's "Orchid Paragraphs"

Teaching Strategies/Sequences

- Invite artist to classroom.
- Rotate small groups of students to work hands on with the visiting artist.
- Artist demonstrates drawing technique (first with pencil) of an orchid still life using new visual arts vocabulary throughout. Artist demonstrates how to add color, perspective, shading, balance, etc.
- Students create own drawings based on step-by-step guidance of the artist (ELL and special learner accommodation).
- Students orally recount what they learned (art vocabulary, techniques, and steps).
- The next day, create a web of new art vocabulary. Students orally recount what they learned with a partner.
- Students write their own paragraph then discuss, edit, and revise with partner.
- Students confer with teacher and create final draft.
- Display paragraphs with art work. Pair with music for an Open House classroom presentation.
- Visiting artist responds in writing to student's work. Teacher reads his letter to the class.

Assessments/evaluations

Q: How did you evaluate/assess student learning?

Mrs. Laws: I think our assessments of what the students learned were imbedded and infused within the lesson activities. For instance, after the artist demonstration, my students applied that knowledge directly within their individual drawings and paragraphs. Also, they orally recounted their knowledge of new art vocabulary. In other words, they showed what they learned in an active manner through discussion, partner work, drawing, writing, and speaking. Finally, their work was proudly displayed in the class-room, and then we made a PowerPoint slide show of their artwork and their writing. We entitled the slide show "An Art Lesson," and we set it to music and played it for Open House.

l e s s o n   t r a c k e r

Mrs. Laws's "Orchid Paragraphs"

Assessments/Evaluations

- *Students orally recount* steps of drawing techniques using new art terms.
- *Class discussion and partner work* is based on new vocabulary web
- *Authentic assessments*—Students actively apply knowledge of new vocabulary through pro-ducing and displaying individual art work paired with narrative paragraphs

Q: Did this integrated lesson serve to increase intended student learning? Why or why not? How?

Mrs. Laws: This lesson went beyond my expectations. The writing that was produced was incredible even from my special needs students. They all were able to use a great deal of new English language vocabulary (visual art elements and concepts) within their paragraphs. Also, they were willing to write more because of all the discussion and hands-on reference. Because of this, their writing was more interesting. This class had trouble in the past with staying on topic and writing cohesive sentences that flowed from one thought to the next. I anticipated several rough drafts but that wasn't the case. They all had so much to say, and they were bringing in other staff members to check out their work (PE teacher, librarian, administration, and just about anyone they met).

• BEYOND THE CLASSROOM

Locate Resources Beyond Your Classroom

Visit your local museums, arts venues and arts educational programs, historical societies, community landmarks, and cultural centers to see what resources are available to students, families, and teachers to extend learning through the arts. Ask about information of interest to K–8 students and their families as well as artist-in-residence programs, field trips, and visitors to school sites. One example of an arts education provider is "Young Audiences." See www.youngaudiences.com for a directory of information near you.

Arts Infusion in Action: Classroom Vignettes

Reflections on Mrs. Laws's lesson.   In this vignette, Mrs. Laws chose to utilize an important "outside the classroom" resource: someone she knew (her father) acting as a guest teacher to demonstrate visual art techniques. However, the planning and sequencing of this lesson was completely *her own* vision. She learned that her idea was a good one and that her plan for hands-on arts-activity infusion served to increase writing and oral language skills in her classroom. She could see the results, as could students, parents, administrators, and others. This was a memorable learning experience for all.

Mrs. Law's classroom example may also provoke other questions, perhaps related to darker truths we may not want to verbalize. For example, some of you may be wondering how, in light of the considerable and sometimes overwhelming demands of standardized testing, Mrs. Laws actually had the time (and permission) to plan and implement an integrated arts activity into her regular classroom literacy instruction? Others may be wondering if what Mrs. Laws accomplished must require the unique talents of a visiting artist guest or particularly high-achieving students. Others of you may feel her integrated lesson was interesting but had nothing to do with your curriculum challenges or future challenges in X content area(s) of grade X. Some of these concerns can be answered now, and others will be addressed throughout this book.

Mrs. Laws is one of many real-life, practicing inner-city K–8 classroom teachers you will meet and get to know throughout this book. Their schools are Title I schools with 100 percent of the students qualifying for free lunch programs. (Well over 90 percent of these children are English language learners.) The overwhelming majority of the ideas you will read do *not* require an arts specialist or specialized arts background to teach, and all were created and taught by the teachers themselves.

Considerations in Mrs. Laws's planning and teaching.   Mrs. Laws took the time to think of, plan, teach, display, extend student learning, and reflect upon and evaluate her customized, integrated lesson. She did so because she and others like her have determined (through direct experience) that the arts *enliven* and *enhance* student learning within content area instruction. Research clearly indicates arts activities can and do provide increased avenues for student participation, active involvement, meaning making, and memory of the learning at hand (Cornett, 2006;

1.5   Resource Suggestion

For age-appropriate, classroom-teacher-friendly, standards-based, integrated arts activities (including all four arts) tied to music and language/literacy development and across the grades 1–6 curriculum, see teacher text and CD series (with extra materials and visual arts transparencies for classroom use) in *Making Music with the Arts and Across the Curriculum* (Grades 1–6) by Pearson Education, Silver Burdett Music (2008).

Fiske, 1999, Hancock, 2007; Jensen, 2005; McDonald & Fisher, 2002, 2006; Smith, 2001).

Mrs. Laws's lesson did require some *focused thinking, reflection,* and *comprehensive curriculum planning toward student understanding* (Posner, 1995; Wiggins & McTighe, 2006). All good teaching requires the same. She had to:

- First *identify* her literacy instruction needs or "big picture" teaching goals linked to content standards.
- *Know what her students needed to know* and then be willing to seek "doable" arts activity to successfully pair with those carefully identified needs.
- *Imagine* what she wanted to happen during the lesson (toward her standards-based content goals). In her particular case, Mrs. Laws looked outside her classroom walls for resources, that is, asked what a guest artist could add to her lesson.
- *Be willing to experiment* (and even fail), to learn along with her students during an integrated arts activity. Accommodations for student needs were made during visual art instruction.
- *Utilize that increased learning* to encourage students to *learn more* and *do more* descriptive paragraph writing.
- *Create a formal or informal display piece or opportunity,* a form of performance art (authentic assessment) through a PowerPoint slide show paired with recorded music for audience viewing at a school Open House. Others were able to see what the students did and learned.
- *Acknowledge what she (the teacher) learned* through watching and reflecting on what happened with her students.
- *Use what she learned to improve her future teaching.* Mrs. Laws's literacy content instruction was consequently enhanced and augmented by this reflective practice experience. Pride in the successful results served as a motivation to incorporate more of these kinds of arts-infused activities into her classroom curriculum.

Many of you would like to involve more of your future or current students in arts activities to establish and increase important learning connections throughout their school-day curriculum and experiences. You may feel you also need some time and guidance to think, plan, and teach (or learn to teach) in more creative, engaging, and productive ways.

Through reading Mrs. Laws's classroom example, debriefing, and discussion, you have begun to explore the potential benefits of designing your own arts-infused lesson ideas across the curriculum. That process includes customized standards-based curriculum planning; experimental teaching through arts infusion, evaluation, and assessment; and self-reflection.

With these important goals in mind, let's consider another arts-infused lesson example from a middle school social studies/U.S. history classroom.

● IN THE CLASSROOM

Integrating Social Studies/U.S. History with the Arts: "Let's Find Out: George Washington and the American Revolutionary War" Content Areas: Middle School History/Social Science, English Language Arts, Arts (Theatre, Music, Visual Art)

Big ideas tied to content standards. Mr. Gonzalez wanted his middle school history/social studies students (grade 8) to know and remember more standards-based facts about George Washington and the American Revolutionary War. First, he asked his class what they already knew about George Washington. He listed their ideas ("He's important!" "His picture is on the one-dollar bill," "Washington, D.C., was named after him."). The students were then asked what they knew about American Revolutionary War ("The British soldiers wore red," "The Americans won!").

● l e s s o n   t r a c k e r

Mr. Gonzalez's "Let's Find Out: George Washington and the American Revolutionary War"

Big Ideas
Who was George Washington, and what was the American Revolutionary war? Find out what the students already know and what they want to know about the topic. Formulate questions and research activities based on student input.

Content Standards Addressed

- **Grade 8: U.S. History and Geography**—Understand major events preceding the founding of the nation; understand the role of leaders such as George Washington.

- **Grade 8: English Language Arts**—Read and respond to historically or culturally significant works of literature that reflect and enhance their studies of history and social science; deliver oral responses to literature

- **Grade 8: Theatre**—Use theatrical skills to present content or concepts in other subject areas; write and create short dramatizations; perform character-based improvisations, pantomimes, or monologues.

- **Grade 8: Music**—Understand the historical contributions and cultural dimensions of music; identify and explain the influences of various cultures on music in early U.S. history; perform music from diverse genres, cultures, and time periods.

Students were then asked what *they* wanted to learn about each of the categories (Washington and the American Revolutionary War), and their ideas were listed on the board in the form of questions (e.g., Who was in the American Army? Were young people involved? What weapons did they use? etc.) *Mr. Gonzalez used these student questions to formulate what the students needed to know.*

● l e s s o n   t r a c k e r

Mr. Gonzalez's "Let's Find Out: George Washington and the American Revolutionary War" (cont.)

Considerations/Steps in Planning

● By asking his students what they already knew about the topic, Mr. Gonzalez found out his students' knowledge was very limited.

● Mr. Gonzalez designed his integrated lesson based on what the students wanted to learn about the topic. He solicited questions from his students and used those questions as points of inquiry to shape their small-group research project.

● In order to further involve the students in the topic, Mr. Gonzalez found and used biographical texts, reader's theatre, dramatized scenes from historical and informational texts, visual art, and music (based on the historical period).

● Mr. Gonzalez wanted the students to create and present their small-group research using multiple forms of media.

Teaching strategies/sequences. Mr. Gonzalez found a short biography of George Washington and prepared a simple scripted reader's theatre based on selected parts of the book's text. On another day, Mr. Gonzalez helped students dramatize short scenes about General George Washington described in the book text and in their history textbook.

The students learned to sing "Yankee Doodle" with a CD recording of the song using song sheets (see Figure 1.2, "Music and Words to 'Yankee Doodle'" on p. 20). Students learned the meaning of the original song text through participation in a reader's theatre (see Figure 1.3, "Yankee Doodle Reader's Theatre" on p. 21). The school music teacher lent Mr. Gonzalez a state-adopted K–8 music textbook series (Pearson Education/Silver Burdett's "Making Music, K–8," 2005) that provides a CD recording of the song paired with a historical painting of two young men playing the fife (small wooden flute) and drum as they march with the American soldiers.

1.6 More about American Patriotic Songs

For more information, background, and history of famous U.S. patriotic songs, see the following sources:

Cohn, A. (Ed.). (1993). *From sea to shining sea: A treasury of American folklore and folk songs.* New York: Scholastic

Collins, A. (2003). *Songs sung red, white, and blue: The stories behind America's best-loved patriotic songs.* New York: HarperCollins.

Arts Infusion in Action: Classroom Vignettes

FIGURE 1.2 Music and words to "Yankee Doodle" from Grade 2, Pupil's Edition (p. 405) of *Making Music* K–8 by Pearson Education/ Silver Burdett Music. © 2005. Used by permission.

The middle school students were very curious about both General Washington, his soldiers, and the young musicians.

● BEYOND THE CLASSROOM

Adopted Text Series in K–8 Music

To locate your district's state/national adopted text series (books and CDs) in music, ask your university music or arts methods instructors or the librarian, principal, and/or vice principal at your school site. Practicing teachers can also visit your district resource center or talk to any music teachers and/or district visual and performing arts coordinators.

The next day, Mr. Gonzalez assigned "Let's Find Out" groups: small groups of students, each selecting one of the questions posed by the entire class at the beginning of the unit. (Remember that these questions were based on what students wanted to know about the topic.) The student groups were encouraged to use their history texts, websites, school

Reader #1: Songs have a history and their words tell an ever-changing story. Today, Americans are known as "Yankees" all over the world and our song "Yankee Doodle Dandy" is sung, played, and enjoyed by people everywhere.

Reader #2: The song "Yankee Doodle" has a long and very funny history. It has been popular in America and around the world for more than 200 years. The original tune was heard in England in the 1600s and was originally known as "Nancy Dawson." Then the song took on new forms and became known as "Nankey Doodle."

Reader #3: A "Nankey" was a Puritan, a member of a group of people who questioned and rejected traditional British government and religious establishments. The song makes fun of these people as slow and simple-minded. Puritans, as we know, eventually settled in America at Plymouth Rock and beyond, so the tradition of making fun of them continued during colonial times. Little did anyone know what would happen to this song and a nation about to be born.

Reader #4: There is a popular legend that when the Native Americans first met the Puritan settlers they had trouble pronouncing the word "English." Instead, the natives used the slang word "Nankey" in referring to the Puritan settlers but actually pronounced the word as "Yankee." So, eventually the British began to sing the words "Yankee Doodle" instead. The story goes on . . .

Reader #5: The man who wrote the words we know today was Dr. Richard Shuckburgh, a surgeon in the British Army stationed in the American colonies during the Revolutionary War. He wrote the words to "Yankee Doodle" to make fun of the poor American troops, their ragged clothes, carefree attitudes, disorganization, and lack of traditional British military discipline and training.

Reader #6: The words "thick as hasty pudding" actually meant the American soldiers were very disorganized and slow. A "dandy" was a person who acted more important than he really was, and the American soldiers were said to be more interested in dancing, music, and fun than the British soldiers of the time.

Reader #7: Captain Washington (George Washington) seemed to be giving a few too many orders to his men. . . . "I guess there was a million." We all know that in another popular version of the song, someone seemed have had a pony named "Macaroni," which seems to be pretty close to our slang for "noodle brained"! A "macaroni" was actually a knot located around a hat brim where people placed a feather.

Reader #8: The Americans surprised the British and adopted the song "Yankee Doodle" as their very own. The song became a source of great Colonial pride. They loved the humor and the tune so much, they ended up singing, marching, whistling, and playing the fife and drum to "Yankee Doodle" wherever they went.

Reader #9: In fact, when the British troops surrendered, the British general, Lord Cornwallis, paraded his well-dressed troops to meet the American general, George Washington. Thousands of Americans looked on. When Lord Cornwallis handed over his sword (a signal of official surrender), George Washington gave a signal. The American band began playing "Yankee Doodle" as loudly as they could.

Reader #10: We wonder if it was the Americans' way of making fun of the British right back by actually enjoying and adopting a song meant to make fun of them. Maybe that's the best thing to do when people make fun of us!

FIGURE 1.3 Yankee Doodle Reader's Theatre

Source: From *Teaching Literacy through the Arts*, (p. 94), by N. L. McDonald and D. Fisher, 2006, New York: Guilford. Reprinted with permission.

Arts Infusion in Action: Classroom Vignettes

library books, interviews with teachers and parents or grandparents, videos and DVDs, and any other sources they could find to collect historical/factual information answering the research question they selected.

Two days later, Mr. Gonzalez invited small groups to share what they found out. Finally, based on what the small groups discovered, the class created an illustrated, fact-based class bulletin board, "All About George Washington and the American Revolutionary War."

lesson tracker

Mr. Gonzalez's "Let's Find Out: George Washington and the American Revolutionary War"

Teaching Strategies/Sequences

- Ask what students already know about the topic, and record what they want to know in the form of questions.
- Use informational text (biography) to create a scripted reader's theatre. Use history textbook information to help students write and create their own dramatized historical scenes, dialogues, and movement tableaux based on the topic and perform them for class, then analyze how historical facts were portrayed.
- Show historical paintings and song text from this period and analyze with entire class. Decode historical song text meaning and analyze historical settings of paintings. Perform music of the period.
- Use original student questions. Assign research project to small groups based on answering one question offered earlier in the unit.
- Have small groups share what they found out. Class creates a fact-based bulletin board display using input from all the groups' research.

Assessments/evaluations. As you just read, Mr. Gonzalez constructed his integrated unit around what his students *needed to know* in order to master content outlined in History/Social Science standards. He then searched resources at the school site library (and with the music teacher) to provide catalysts for creative arts-related activities linked to the facts his students needed to know.

Through experimentation within active student learning contexts (*doing* a reader's theatre, *creating* historic fact-based reenactments, *singing* song texts and *viewing and discussing* art), Mr. Gonzalez was able to *authentically assess* increased student interest, involvement, and memory of the learning at hand (Eisner, 1980; Frey & Fisher, 2007; Frey,

Fisher, & Moore 2005; Gardner, 1984, 1993a, 1993b; Jacobs, 1989, 1997; Jensen, 2005; McDonald & Fisher, 2002, 2006; Rosenblatt, 1995).

• l e s s o n   t r a c k e r

Mr. Gonzalez's "Let's Find Out: George Washington and the American Revolutionary War"

Assessments/Evaluation

- Mr. Gonzalez assessed what his students already knew and wanted to know about the topic through class discussion. This informal assessment shaped the content of the unit.

- Student script writing and dramatic presentations of historical scenes were measured/graded for accuracy of content, use of historical facts, and vocabulary.

- Authentic assessments/rubrics—Students' dramatic scenes, oral presentations of "Let's Find Out" facts, were graded on a scale of 1 to 5 using a rubric. The rubric included the following categories: preparation, organization, clarity of speech/presentation style, met the goal of answering the research question, historical accuracy, creativity.

Reflections on Mr. Gonzalez's lesson.   Mr. Gonzalez offered the following:

> This kind of integrated teaching is new to me, but well worth the effort it took. I experimented with asking students what *they already knew and what they wanted to know.* By them telling me (and me listening to their responses), I was able to create some simple ways to incorporate arts activity (theatre, music, and visual art) into their inquiry. I'm not talented, believe me, but I tried it anyway! They wanted to *do* the activities because it was a way for them to answer their own questions, be creative, and see and enjoy the end results of their study. They felt they were a part of the history they were studying. Their memory of the historical facts and events of this time period increased achievement on both class assessments, and standardized tests far exceeding the achievement of previous years. Now my only problem is that my students are always asking me when we are going to "do" things again with whatever we are learning.

Importantly, throughout this unit, Mr. Gonzalez deliberately and creatively addressed multiple learning styles and made important connections across content areas through student participation in active arts activities (Gardner, 1993a, 1993b; Harmin, 1994; Jacobs, 1989). What Mr. Gonzalez's middle school students describe as "fun because we got to do things" is actually evidence of increased participation, learning, and memory of their learning about George Washington and the American Revolutionary War.

Conclusion

The arts are, by law, core content, worthy of study unto themselves. Yet, with the challenges of delivering standards-based, specialized instruction in all four arts to *all* students, something else is needed. Future and practicing classroom teachers may desire to and do successfully use the arts within content instruction across the curriculum as a way to teach more students with and through the expressive and memorable learning avenues the arts provide.

Within this chapter's real-life classroom examples, both Mrs. Laws and Mr. Gonzalez offered powerful insights into how they planned, taught, and evaluated their customized arts-infused lessons. Finally, through your reading, you have begun to think about your own arts-infused teaching and the planning processes involved.

References

Armstrong, T. (2003). *The multiple intelligences of reading and writing: Making the words come alive.* Alexandria, VA: Association for Supervision and Curriculum Development.

Arts Education Partnership. (2002). *Critical links: Learning in the arts and student academic and social development.* Washington, DC: Council of Chief State School Officers.

Barrett, J. (2001). Interdisciplinary work and musical integrity. *Music Educators Journal, 87*(5), 27–31.

Barrett, J., McCoy, C., & Veblen, K. (1997). *Sound ways of knowing: Music in the interdisciplinary curriculum.* New York: Schirmer Books.

Barry, N. (1998). Arts integration in the elementary classroom: Conference development and evaluation. *Update: Applications of Research in Music Education, 17*(1), 3–8.

California Department of Education. (1996). *Visual and performing arts framework for California public schools: Kindergarten through grade twelve.* Sacramento: California Department of Education.

Cohn, A. (Ed.). (1993). *From sea to shining sea: A treasury of American folklore and folk songs.* New York: Scholastic.

Collins, A. (2003). *Songs sung red, white, and blue: The stories behind America's best-loved patriotic songs.* New York: Harper-Collins.

Consortium of National Arts Education Associations. (1994). *Dance, music, theatre, visual arts: What every young American should know and be able to do in the arts: National standards for arts education.* Reston, VA: Music Educators National Conference.

Cornett, C. (2006). *Creating meaning through literature and the arts: An integration resource for classroom teachers* (3rd ed.). Upper Saddle River, NJ: Prentice Hall.

Eisner, E. (1980). The arts as a way of knowing. *Principal, 60*(1), 11–14.

Fiske, E. (Ed.). (1999). *Champions of change: The impact of the arts on learning.* Washington, DC: The Arts Education Partnership and the President's Committee on the Arts and the Humanities.

Frey, N., & Fisher, D. (2007). *Reading for information in elementary school: Content literacy strategies to build comprehension.* Upper Saddle River, NJ: Merrill/Prentice Hall.

Frey, N., Fisher, D., & Moore, K. (2005). *Designing responsive curriculum: Planning lessons that work.* Lanham, MD: Rowman & Littlefield.

Gardner, H. (1984). *Art, mind and brain: A cognitive approach to creativity.* New York: Basic Books.

Gardner, H. (1993a). *Frames of mind: The theory of multiple intelligences* (Tenth Anniversary Edition). New York: Basic Books.

Gardner, H. (1993b). *Multiple intelligences: The theory in practice.* New York: Basic Books.

Gelineau, R. (2003). *Integrating the arts across the elementary school curriculum.* Belmont, CA: Wadsworth.

Hancock, M. (2007). *A celebration of literature and response: Children, books, and teachers in K–8 classrooms* (3rd ed.). Upper Saddle River, NJ: Prentice Hall.

Harmin, M. (1994). *Inspiring active learning: A handbook for teachers.* Alexandria, VA: Association for Supervision and Curriculum Development.

Jacobs, H. H. (1989). *Interdisciplinary curriculum: Design and implementation.* Alexandria, VA: Association for Supervision and Curriculum Development.

Jacobs, H. H. (1997). *Mapping the big picture: Integrating curriculum and assessment K-12.* Alexandria, VA: Association for Supervision and Curriculum Development.

Jensen, E. (2005). *Arts with the brain in mind* (2nd ed.). Alexandria, VA: Association for Supervision and Curriculum Development.

Leonard, C. (1991). *The status of arts education in American public schools.* Urbana: National Arts Education Research Center at the University of Illinois.

Marzano. R. J. (2004). *Building background knowledge for academic achievement: Research on what works in schools.* Alexandria, VA: Association for Supervision and Curriculum Development.

McDonald, N. (2008). Standards in the arts and arts within literacy instruction. In J. Flood, S. Brice-Heath, & D. Lapp (Eds.), *The Handbook of Research on Teaching Literacy Through the Communicative, Performing, and Visual Arts Volume II: Sponsored by the International Reading Association.* Mahwah, NJ: Lawrence Erlbaum.

McDonald, N., & Fisher, D. (2002). *Developing arts-loving readers: Top 10 questions teachers are asking about integrated arts education.* Lanham, MD, and London: Rowman & Littlefield Education.

McDonald, N., & Fisher, D. (2006). *Teaching literacy through the arts.* New York: Guilford.

Pearson Education/Silver Burdett Music. (2005). *Making music K–8 (National Text and CD Series in Music).* Parsippany, NJ: Pearson Education.

Pearson Education/Silver Burdett Music (2008). *Making music with the arts and across the curriculum (grades 1–6).* (CD and Books). Parsippany, NJ: Pearson Education.

Posner, G. (1995). *Analyzing the curriculum* (2nd ed.). New York: McGraw-Hill.

Rosenblatt, L. (1995). *Literature as exploration.* New York: Modern Language Association.

Smith, S. (2001). *The power of the arts: Creative strategies for teaching exceptional learners.* Baltimore, MD: Brookes.

Snyder, S. (2001). Connection, correlation, and integration. *Music Educators Journal, 87*(5), 32–39.

Spenser, S., Wachowiak, S., Fisher, D., & Pumpian, I. (Eds.). (2005). *Challenging the classroom standard through museum-based education.* New York: Lawrence Erlbaum.

Stake, R., Bresler, L., & Mabry, L. (1991). *Custom and cherishing: The arts in elementary schools.* Urbana: National Arts Education Research Center at the University of Illinois.

Wiggins, G., & McTighe, J. (2006). *Understanding by design* (2nd ed.). Alexandria, VA: Association for Supervision and Curriculum Development.

chapter 2

What Students Need to Know

To begin with the end in mind means to start with a clear understanding of your destination. It means to know where you're going so that you better understand where you are now so that the steps you take are always in the right direction.

—Stephen R. Covey (*The Seven Habits of Highly Effective People,* 1989, p. 98)

FOCUS ACTIVITY

Directions: Please fill out before and after reading this chapter.

Before Reading Chapter A = agree D = disagree	Statements	After Reading Chapter A = agree D = disagree
	There are areas of (and content students need to know within) curriculum that could benefit from arts-activity infusion.	
	I am able to imagine what arts activities I would use in arts-infused lessons across the curriculum.	
	Pre-planning and linking arts activities to big ideas and content standards will take a great deal of effort and time.	
	I am concerned that I am not artistically talented and it will adversely affect my planning for arts-infused lessons.	

2.1 Resource about Lesson Design

For more comprehensive information, designs, and techniques for constructivist curriculum planning and lesson design (based on "what students need to know" through "backward design" with "big idea" teaching goals in mind, see *Understanding by Design* (expanded second edition) by Grant Wiggins and Jay McTighe (2006, Merrill/Prentice Hall).

In this chapter, you will become familiar with our K–8 contributing teachers' initial stage of purposeful planning with the arts. Through their examples, standards-based content area big ideas of what students need to know and be able to do will be discussed. These content goals then become paired (infused) within ideas for appropriate standards-based arts activities. Finally, you will be guided through a self-study exercise and reflective peer discussion designed to help you develop initial plans for your own arts-infused lesson(s).

Food for Thought: What Your Students Need to Know

During the initial stage of your own purposeful planning, first focus on *what students need know* within your classroom or future classroom curriculum (Wiggins & McTighe, 2006). Let the following questions serve as food for thought:

- What "big ideas" in your curriculum do your students or future students need to know and be able to do? Why?

- Which of these needs seem to lend themselves to arts-infused lessons linked to content area instruction? Why?

- Which arts should I seek to include? Why?

- What are some ways I think I might use/link arts activities within a selected lesson?

- How do I think these kinds of arts activities might enrich my teaching and student understanding? Why?

- By the end of an imagined lesson using the arts within a content lesson, what will students be able to know and do?

- Finally, what do I hope to accomplish or have happen during this lesson?

Hints for Reading Contributing Teacher Examples

You are about to read the initial planning stages of one lesson from each of our K–8 classroom teacher contributors. Throughout the book you will read how these particular lessons developed and evolved through several purposeful planning stages.

Here, it is extremely important to mention the natural human tendency to be primarily interested in lessons directly linked to the grade-level content we actually teach or plan to teach. You may also be tied to your own state's particular content standards. The exact language of content standards in this book's examples and "Lesson Tracker" boxes may vary from what you already know and use or have begun to study and use in methods classes.

However, in order to gain the most from what is offered here, you may need to open your mind the panorama of ideas these real-life examples can provide. Consider all examples as food for thought, even if an example may be at a grade level much lower or higher than your current or future grade level or content area. Furthermore, an example lesson with content from a different grade level can often spark an idea appropriate to your own situation.

> ### 2.2 Record Your Ideas
>
> **Ideas for your own use will come to you as you read our teacher contributors' plans:** Use sticky notes and jot down your own translations of ideas that might be appropriate and effective within your own or future classroom. Remember that an idea in middle school math, for example, may give you an idea for another content area at a much different grade level.

● BEYOND THE CLASSROOM ....

Find out where arts resources are:

In your methods class or at grade-level or other on-site teacher meetings, ask what peers are already doing with the arts within their curriculum. Find out who uses music, visual art, theatre, or dance within their teaching, and ask them to share their ideas and resources with you. Where are arts-related materials and supplies located at your university library, on-line, and/or at school-site and district resource centers?

K–8 Teacher Contributors: First Stages of Purposeful Planning

As you read the following examples, note the incredible variety of approaches and the different ways our teachers describe their student needs and plans for using the

Grouchy, happy, lonely, beautiful, quiet insects by Ms. Tanonis's K/1 class.

Photo by Rose Tanonis.

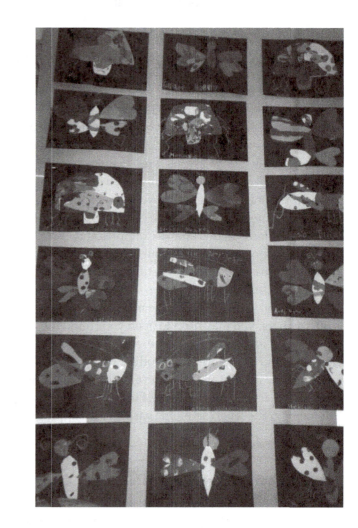

arts. Let's investigate what our K–8 classroom teacher contributors thought about as they, too, were in the initial planning stages of one of the lessons you will revisit throughout this book.

Integrating Science and the Arts: "Lifecycle of Butterflies" Content Areas: Science, English Language Arts (Reading/Author Study, Oral Language), Arts (Visual Art)

Ms. Rose Tanonis teaches a K/1 combination class at an inner-city elementary school. One of her lesson/unit ideas has a science focus, on the life cycle of butterflies. In it, she wants also to connect to literacy and language arts through the use of a book and artist/author study of *The Very Hungry Caterpillar* by Eric Carle (1994, Hamlish Hamilton).

Big ideas tied to content standards. According to Ms. Tanonis, the "big ideas" her students need to know and be able to do in Science involve the following:

● Understand the life cycle of a butterfly

● Learn and recognize external features of insects

In addition, Ms. Tanonis wants to establish the following Visual Art connections and feels her students need to know and be able to do the following in that Art:

● Create artwork based on observations of actual objects

● Use texture in two-dimensional works of art

● Discuss works of art created in the classroom

● Identify and describe various reasons for making art

● l e s s o n   t r a c k e r

Ms. Tanonis's "Lifecycle of Butterflies"
Content Standards Addressed
(K/1)

Science: Life Science and Investigation/Experimentation

● Know how to identify major structures of common plants and animals (e.g., stems, leaves, roots, arms, wings, legs).

● Communicate observations orally and through drawings.

● Know that the sequential stages of life cycles are different for different animals, such as butterflies, frogs, and mice.

Language Arts: Oral Language/Literary Response

- Share information and ideas.
- Describe people, places, things (e.g., size, color, shape), locations, and actions.
- Describe the roles of authors and illustrators and their contributions to print materials.

Visual Art

- Identify the elements of art (line, color, shape/form, texture, value, space) in the environment and in works of art, emphasizing line, color, and shape/form.
- Discuss the various works of art that artists create and the types of media used.
- Use texture in two-dimensional and three-dimensional works of art. Demonstrate beginning skill in the manipulation and use of sculptural materials (clay, paper, and papier mâché) to create form and texture in works of art.
- Discuss works of art created in the classroom, focusing on selected elements of art (e.g., shape/form, texture, line, color).

Purposeful planning goals. By the end of her unit on insects, Ms. Tanonis wants her students to

> learn the different parts of insects and what makes an insect an insect. I want my students to describe works of art created in the classroom and identify and describe various reasons for making art. The children will learn aesthetic valuing. They will learn about the author (Eric Carle) and become familiar with his literature and art.
>
> I want my lessons to get the children to start talking about their artwork and use words like *shape/form, texture, line, color,* etc. I want the children to apply what they learned about insects to elements in art such as the lines, textures, shapes, colors, and forms.
>
> I hope to accomplish an engaging unit that incorporates several curriculum standards. I want the children to learn about insects and their parts that make them unique. I want them to enjoy an author study and learn Eric Carle's art medium. I think I want my students to make paper, add texture to it through paint, make templates of the insects, and create their individual artwork.

Discussion. Ms. Tanonis shows us that she is *equally* concerned with standards-based student learning needs in both Science and in Visual Art. As such, she is already thinking in a highly integrated fashion about the pairing of what her students need to know in science to an art study and activity based on the work of Eric Carle. The subject of Carle's artwork is directly linked to her science curriculum. His art has given her insights into how visual art activity could be used to teach and reinforce what her students' need to know about insects.

Finally, she hopes that art activity will help "cement" what students need to know in science through creative and engaging avenues designed to enhance student memory of that learning.

• IN THE CLASSROOM

Integrating Math and the Arts: "Singing, Moving, Drawing on the Language of Math" Content Areas: Math, English Language Arts (Reading/Author Study, Oral Language), Arts (Visual Art, Music, Dance)

Mrs. Adrienne Laws teaches second grade in an inner-city school. One of her lessons, "Singing, Moving, Drawing on the Language of Math," involves the creative pairing of music, dance, and visual art to help her students understand and master math word-problem operations. She thoughtfully comments on her initial planning considerations, "Word problems are difficult for

Mrs. Laws's second-grade student presentations in her lesson "Singing, Moving, Drawing on the Language of Math."

Photo by Adrienne Laws.

second language students, especially emergent English readers. I think my students need to be taught to look for key words to figure out what operation to use." Mrs. Laws also notes that her students' musical participation in repeating song texts and movement may be key to their mastery of these math terms and operations linked to developing literacy skills.

Big ideas tied to content standards. The "big ideas" her students need to know in particular math operations include:

- fewer, more, or less = subtract
- and, in all, altogether = add
- greater or left = subtract

  The arts activities she would like to use include:

- Analysis of song lyrics about math operations for vocabulary and comprehension
- Singing with created dance movements
- Illustration of song lyrics (poetry) and out-loud discussion (oral language) of art work
- Performance sharing and displays of student work

l e s s o n   t r a c k e r

Mrs. Laws's "Singing, Moving, Drawing on the Language of Math"
Content Standards Addressed
(Grade Two)

Math Standards
- Understand and use the inverse relationship between addition and subtraction (e.g., an opposite number sentence for $8 + 6 = 14$ is $14 - 6 = 8$) to solve problems and check solutions.
- Relate problem situations to number sentences involving addition and subtraction.

Music Standards
- Sing age-appropriate songs from memory.
- Students apply what they learn in music across subject areas (analysis of song lyrics/meaning).
- Create developmentally appropriate movements to express pitch, tempo, form, and dynamics in music.

Dance Standards
- Create and improvise movement patterns and sequences.

Visual Art Standards
- Create a painting or drawing

Purposeful planning goals. By the end of this lesson, Mrs. Laws wants her students to "find important information, locate key words, and know what math operation to use when seeing word problems." She goes on to explain, "By learning a song that repeats key terms and then putting movement to the lyrics, students are more apt to remember the addition and subtraction terms and operations."

Mrs. Laws concludes, "Besides the aforementioned, pairs of students will create artwork for each math term and share with the whole group. We will sort the words and keep them posted as a reference in the classroom, adding to it as we learn more key terminology throughout the year."

Discussion. In her purposeful planning, Mrs. Laws has paired what she knows to be her students' needs in mastering math terms with what music, dance, and visual art activities may offer to reinforce that particular learning. She seems to have created or found an appropriate song to use in her lesson. Mrs. Laws views the innate repetition of oral language (use of math terms in fluency) found within an engaging song text about math operations to be an effective and natural way for her students to learn. She also seeks to include total physical response through movement, thereby kinesthetically reinforcing student understanding of the song lyrics. Furthermore, she intends to infuse visual art (thematic illustration) as a way for students to create their own interpretations of featured math terms to share out loud with others. Mrs. Laws wants to incorporate cooperative learning (pairs), informal performance sharing, and classroom displays as active and authentic ways to assess students' participation, engagement, and memory of what they need to know.

• IN THE CLASSROOM

Integrating Social Studies (Geography) and the Arts:
"Desert Habitat Art" Content Areas: History/Social Science (Geography), Arts (Visual Art)

Mrs. Kate Gray teaches grade 3 at an inner-city school. She is planning a series of thematic, integrated lessons about "Where Living Things Are Found." One of her lessons within this theme centers around both Social Studies (Geography) and Science (Life Science) content in a lesson called "Desert Habitat Art." Mrs. Gray seeks to infuse visual art activities (on-location sketching and, later, watercolor media) into her social studies/science lesson because she "hopes my students will take their understanding to a deeper level."

In a succinct manner (one that resonates for many of us), Mrs. Gray simply states, "My instructional focus was determined by our state content standards and a grade-level decision to teach specific standards at this time of the year."

Mrs. Gray's students sketching outdoors in the beautiful Cactus Garden in Balboa Park, San Diego, California.

Photo by Kate Gray.

Big ideas tied to content standards. The "big idea" in Social Studies that her students need to know is:

- Students need to understand landforms (desert)

   "Big ideas" in Science include:

- Students need to learn concepts of desert environments and habitats.

- Students need to understand ecosystems (desert).

Mrs. Gray wants to use Visual Art activities to:

- Create (on-location/live) landscape sketches and watercolor paintings that will integrate students' understanding of habitats (desert).

- Help students learn new visual art media (watercolor) as they explore concepts of foreground, middle ground, and background and perspective as they create landscape paintings.

● l e s s o n   t r a c k e r

Mrs. Gray's "Desert Habitat Art"

Content Standards Addressed

(Grade Three)

History/Social Science

● Students identify and describe physical geography and use a variety of ways to organize information about people, places and environments in a spatial context.

● Students identify geographical features in their local region (desert environment).

Science

● Students know plants and animals have structures that serve different functions in growth, survival, and reproduction.

● Students know examples of diverse life forms in different environments, such as oceans, deserts, tundra, forests, grasslands, and wetlands.

Visual Art

● Students perceive and respond to works of art, objects in nature, events, and the environment. They also use the vocabulary of the visual arts to express their observations.

● Students apply what they learn in the visual arts across subject areas.

● Create a work of art based on the observation of objects and scenes in daily life. Paint or draw a landscape, seascape, or cityscape that shows the illusion of space.

● Identify and describe how foreground, middle ground, and background are used to create the illusion of space.

● Students apply artistic processes and skills, using a variety of media to communicate meaning and intent in original works of art.

Purposeful planning goals. Mrs. Gray's overall goals connect us back to the original social studies/science content focus of her lesson. "I want my students to synthesize their understanding of habitats and landforms in order to create their art work." Her plan is to have students sketch outdoors during a visit to the desert garden at a local city park.

Discussion. Although we do not at this point know exactly how Mrs. Gray will incorporate visual art within her lesson, we do know she will remain focused on her social studies and science content to reinforce what her students need to know. She instinctively knows (through experience) that her students learn and remember more when they are engaged in creative and expressive,

2.3   How about Science?

Be thinking of some science content themes that may lend themselves to an arts-infused lesson. Share these ideas with peers.

hands-on projects. This knowledge may serve as a creative catalyst for her to further develop the visual art activity within this social studies/science–focused lesson.

BEYOND THE CLASSROOM

Teaching Materials

Teacher supply stores and bookstores with educational materials for K–8 students and teachers may provide a wealth of resources for ways to use arts activities at home, in school, and in varied learning environments. One great resource for science ideas at the elementary level is Science Art: Projects and Activities That Teach Science Concepts and Develop Process Skills by Deborah Schecter (1997, Scholastic)

IN THE CLASSROOM

Integrating Social Studies (History/Geography), Math, and the Arts: "Exploration/Colonization" Content Areas: History/Social Science, Math, Arts (Visual Art)

Mr. Khanh Pham has taught grade 5 and currently teaches grade 4 at an inner-city school. He started his school year with a 4/5 combination class, but then (due to enrollment shifts) was assigned a new fourth-grade class in the second month of the school year. Mr. Pham has found this change challenging, but continues to develop new ideas for arts-infused teaching at his new grade level.

One of his ideas centers on the social studies/geography/history theme of "Exploration/Colonization." Mr. Pham seeks to pair social studies content with math skills using a visual art activity. "This activity will help students better identify the early land and sea routes of explorers to North America. Explorers include Captain James Cook, Vitus Bering, and Juan Cabrillo."

Big Ideas tied to content standards. His "big ideas about what his students need to know in Social Studies include the following:

- Identify the European nations.
- Identify European settlements in North America.
- Note importance of settlement locations.
- Describe factors for placement and function of settlements.

His initial ideas involve the inclusion of Visual Art *and* Math skill activities in the following ways:

Mr. Pham's grade 4/5 "Exploration/Colonization" lesson: Settlements were established based on the available resources in the region. This relief map allows students to easily identify those areas.

Photo by Khanh Pham.

- Planning, creating, and constructing labeled maps with physical features of exploration routes
- Discussing and sharing artwork to aid group comprehension, identification, and application to other locations and exploration periods

lesson tracker

Mr. Pham's "Exploration/Colonization"
Content standards addressed
(Grade 4)

History/Social Science
- Identify the early land and sea routes to, and European settlements in, California with a focus on the exploration of the North Pacific (e.g., by Captain James Cook, Vitus Bering, Juan Cabrillo), noting especially the importance of mountains, deserts, ocean currents, and wind patterns.

- Describe the social, political, cultural, and economic life and interactions among people of California from the Pre-Columbian societies to the Spanish Missions and Mexican Rancho periods.

Visual Art

- Visual Literacy—Construct diagrams, maps, graphs, timelines, and illustrations to communicate ideas or tell a story about a historical event.

Purposeful planning goals. By the end of his lesson on exploration and colonization, Mr. Pham clearly wants his students "to be able to describe the social, political, cultural, and economic life and interactions among people of California from the Pre-Columbian societies to the Spanish Missions and Mexican Rancho periods." By infusing a visual art activity, Mr. Pham hopes that his

> students will gain valuable background information that will help them to make conclusions about settlements in California. Furthermore, students can use this information (mapping) to label and identify other physical features associated with California. This lesson will help students identify the impact of European settlements to North America. By mapping the exploration routes, students will be able to develop ideas/reasons for the routes taken by the explorers such as Cabrillo. The physical features of the land (California) help to determine where Europeans settled. As the settlements grow and expand students will be able to identify the available resources of the physical environment.

2.4 Social Studies/History Themes

Be thinking of some **social studies/history** content themes that may lend themselves to an arts-infused lesson. Share these ideas with peers.

Discussion. Here we see that Mr. Pham's lesson is well grounded both in the knowledge of his social studies content (geography/history) as well as in his student's learning needs. He is absolutely clear about what he wants students to learn from their mapping activity. Furthermore, he is also able to focus his planning on his students' future application of the hands-on knowledge they might gain from this arts-infused lesson experience. Furthermore, by thinking ahead, he has built in the creative possibility to continue to use various arts activities within future social studies instruction.

- IN THE CLASSROOM

Integrating Social Studies/History and the Arts: "Jamestown in 1607" Content Areas: History/Social Science, English Language Arts (Writing and Speaking), Arts (Theatre)

Mrs. Colleen Crandall teaches fifth-grade GATE (Gifted and Talented Education) at an inner-city school. While she is aware that her students are exceptional, she has always taught with and through the arts in classes that are not GATE. To her, "It is simply the most effective way to teach . . . hands-on, active learning." One of her lessons, "Jamestown in 1607," uses social studies content infused with literacy/language arts (point-of-view emphasis—writing a reenactment).

Mrs. Crandall chose to connect to the art of theatre to make her lesson come to life. She comments,

> Jamestown was the first colony in the New World and many people don't know this information (compared to what they know about Pilgrims or what people' lives were like during this time in the South). To gain insight into what life was like in Jamestown, I want students to research and reenact a person's life from that time period to "feel" what it was like to live back then.

In Mrs. Crandall's lesson "Jamestown, 1607" students presented originally authored monologues about the life and work of Jamestown trades people.

Photo by Colleen Crandall.

Big Ideas tied to content standards. Mrs. Crandall's "big ideas" her students need to know and "do" in Social Studies are:

- Jobs colonists worked in Jamestown.

- Colonists had to work hard in the new colony to survive and thrive.

- Research and study the various jobs people had and reenact the colonists' jobs for their peers.

   She plans to infuse activities in theatre into her lesson by:

- Script writing and acting linked to characters within what they learned about authentic historical periods and settings

- Characterization through writing from a historical person's perspective and voice

- Acting and performing, analyzing performances for and by peers

BEYOND THE CLASSROOM

Call for Arts Help

If you currently teach or are assisting at a school site, send home a flyer to parents, grandparents, extended family, and guardians soliciting visual art supplies, CDs, books, hats, and costumes, help in the classroom, and guests to share their knowledge and talents in any of the arts.

l e s s o n   t r a c k e r

Mrs. Crandall's "Jamestown in 1607"
Content Standards Addressed
(Grade Five)

History/Social Science Standards
- Students understand the political, religious, social, and economic institutions that evolved in the colonial era.

English Language Arts Standards
- Create multiple-paragraph narrative compositions:
   1. Establish and develop a situation or plot.
   2. Describe the setting.
   3. Present an ending.
- Show, rather than tell, the events of the story.

- Develop the topic with simple facts, details, examples, and explanations.
- Select a focus, organizational structure, and point of view for an oral presentation.
- Clarify and support spoken ideas with evidence and examples.
- Engage the audience with appropriate verbal cues, facial expressions, and gestures.

Theatre Standards

- Interpret how theatre and storytelling forms (past and present) of various cultural groups may reflect their beliefs and traditions.
- Use theatrical skills to dramatize events and concepts from other curriculum areas.

Purposeful planning goals. Specifically, Mrs. Crandall wants her students to know and be able to do the following: "Select a character from this time period and act out a scene from a day in the life of their character to help students in class relate to what life was like in Jamestown at this time."

Her rich commentary about her plans continues,

When students gain a personal "experience" of what life was like during a different time period, they will be able to gain greater understanding of how people lived. "Doing" a colonist's job in a reenactment will create a personal connection to their Jamestown colonist.

I'm hoping my students will write their own scripts by first reading books about Jamestown and learn information about customs, culture, and the technology of this time period. I'd like my students to act out their colonist's point of view of what their life was like. By doing the research on a person and acting it out by sharing this reenactment, I hope my students will more fully experience what life was like during this time period.

Discussion. Mrs. Crandall's first stage of purposeful planning involved a clear desire to make what her students need to know come alive for them and their peers within a final, informal performance sharing. By doing so, she has imagined an authentic assessment (shared performance) of what her students learned. Her focus on activities involving background research, reading, discussion, script writing, and acting based on historical facts will explore Jamestown life in a way that may motivate increased student interest and participation. Her students will know that they have the clearly defined goal of a performance for their peers. This goal will undoubtedly motivate them to make sure that their historical research will come alive in effective, authentic, and understandable ways. Finally, student performances, reflections, and discussions may add considerable depth to their understanding of what they need to know.

● IN THE CLASSROOM

Integrating Math and the Arts: "Measuring and Classifying Angles Through Dance" Content Areas: Math (Measurement and Geometry), Arts (Dance)

Christi Elemont is a teacher of sixth-grade math at an inner-city middle school. In an enthusiastic lesson about "Measuring and Classifying Angles," Ms. Elemont expresses that she "hopes to cover many math standards through dance. I know this could be amazing and could be what they remember and love most!"

Big ideas tied to content standards. Ms. Elemont's "big ideas" of what her students need to know in Math are:

- Classifying angles—acute, obtuse, right
- Measuring angles—Knowing what a specific degree looks like
- Transformations—Reflections and translations

Ms. Elemont's sixth-grade math class performs "Geometry Aerobics" in her lesson "Measuring and Classifying Angles."

Photo by Christi Elemont.

Her Dance activity focus includes:

- Create original group choreography for class performance.
- Use dance in cross-curricular connection with math terminology and physical design and space.

⦿ l e s s o n   t r a c k e r

Ms. Elemont's "Measuring and Classifying Angles through Dance"
Content Standards Addressed
(Grade Six)

Math Standards

- Students identify and describe the properties of two-dimensional figures.
- Identify angles as vertical, adjacent, complementary, or supplementary and provide descriptions of these terms.

Dance Standards

- Demonstrate focus, physical control, coordination, and accurate reproduction in performing locomotor and axial movement.
- Demonstrate the ability to coordinate movement with different musical rhythms and styles.
- Use the elements of dance to create short studies that demonstrate the development of ideas and thematic material.
- Students apply what they learn in dance to learning across subject areas

Purposeful planning goals. Ms. Elemont clearly defines what she wants her students to know and be able to do by the end of these lessons:

- Classify angles
- Know the approximate measures by looking at them
- Know how to translate a figure by actually "doing" reflections, rotations, and transformations (through total body involvement)

    She hopes her students will

    latch on to the material. We'll create a "class dance" and do it throughout the unit. My experience tells me they will ask to perform it over and over again, so maybe that will help with reinforcement also.
        I hope to accomplish success with the math standards through this lesson. It incorporates a massive amount of material from our 6th grade geometry standards and

could be something the children will always remember. In my classroom, I strive to make learning fun and promote student buy-in. This may simply be a lesson activity that will do that.

Discussion. The enthusiasm Ms. Elemont has for her creative lesson idea is infectious. We are left with the feeling that this lesson *will* work because of her positive energy and commitment to meeting her students' needs in new, engaging, and exciting (if not experimental) ways. Ms. Elemont is well aware of her students' needs for total physical involvement (kinesthetic learning) linked to what they need to know about the spatial concepts and terminology related to angles. Through this awareness, she has naturally linked learning in math to learning through dance. Her clear goals and willingness to experiment and create *with* and *for* her students may indeed become successful and memorable learning activities within her math classes.

● IN THE CLASSROOM

Integrating History/Geography and Theatre: "Manifest Destiny: Westward Expansion" Content Areas: History/Social Science, Arts (Theatre)

Mr. Andy Soto teaches eighth-grade U.S. History/Geography in an inner-city middle school. In his classroom content, he chose to link the art of theatre with the idea of "Manifest Destiny: Westward Expansion."

Mr. Soto comments, "The idea of Manifest Destiny is one of our content standards for grade 8. It is important for students to learn how U.S. policy used the ideas of Manifest Destiny to remove Native Americans from the land and acquire land from Mexico."

Big ideas tied to content standards. Mr. Soto lists as the specific "big ideas" his students need to know about Manifest Destiny within U.S. history:

- Differences in economic, political, and social beliefs and practices can lead to division within a nation and have lasting consequences.
- Conflict often brings about great change.
- He hopes to infuse Theatre activities in the following ways:
- Script writing of original plays based on authentic historical information about the topic
- Acting and direction of original plays
- Performance and analysis of plays for and by peers

Mr. Soto's eighth-grade U.S. History students acting out their original play, "When Texas Joined the Union" during their "Westward Expansion" lesson.

Photo by Andy Soto.

lesson tracker

Mr. Soto's "Manifest Destiny: Westward Expansion"

Content Standards Addressed
(Grade 8)

History/Social Science

- Describe the purpose, challenges, and economic incentives associated with westward expansion, including the concept of Manifest Destiny (e.g., the Lewis and Clark expedition, accounts of the removal of Indians, the Cherokees' "Trail of Tears," settlement of the Great Plains) and the territorial acquisitions that spanned numerous decades.

- Describe the Mexican-American War, including territorial settlements, the aftermath of the war, and the effects the war had on the lives of Americans, including Mexican Americans today.

Theatre

- Perform character-based improvisations, pantomimes, or monologues, using voice, blocking, and gesture to enhance meaning.

- Use theatrical skills to present content or concepts in other subjects.

Purposeful planning goals. By the end of this lesson on "Manifest Destiny: Westward Expansion," Mr. Soto wants his students to know the following:

- Understand how the U.S. government used the idea of Manifest Destiny to remove Native Americans from their land
- Understand how "Manifest Destiny" was used to acquire land from Mexico

Based on these goals, Mr. Soto continues, "I think theatre activities will help students learn and remember the concepts being taught. The students will recreate history by performing what they learned. I hope my students will enjoy, laugh, and learn when writing and performing their own plays."

Mr. Soto hopes to accomplish many things during his lesson. (Note the sequential detail in his planning.) He continues,

First, students will predict what sorts of problems the U.S. faced during Westward Expansion. Second, I will provide a brief overview of the main events of the lesson. Students will complete a vocabulary assignment. Third, we will read and analyze a variety of materials about Manifest Destiny and Westward Expansion. Students will take structured notes and complete graphic organizers. Finally, students will write and perform plays which demonstrate what they learned about the Indian removal policies and the war with Mexico.

Discussion. Mr. Soto has not only determined a content theme, but has effectively "mapped out" exactly what he'd like to happen, step by step, in a sequential unit plan based on what his students need to know. You can readily see that he has structured his ideas to suit his own organized teaching style, yet allow for the creative input and time considerations involved with original student writing activity and play production with his middle school students.

Mr. Soto has also matched his purposeful plan to the complex, multifaceted nature of his chosen theme. He has opened himself to the art of theatre to guide him as he allows his students to explore, experiment, and communicate their various unique understandings of Manifest Destiny through their own dramatic interpretations. Theatre, in this case, can serve to heighten and encapsulate our students' individual understandings and portrayals of history, people, and narrative events. In these ways, his students may remember the meaning of Manifest Destiny more readily.

● BEYOND THE CLASSROOM

Find out about displaced groups of people:

Ask your older students or students in the future if they know of groups of people, who, by nature of race, religion, life style, political beliefs, etc., have been displaced or persecuted both in other countries and within our own country. Students may choose to interview family members, friends, and community members to gain various perspectives and narrative information.

The real-life examples of our contributing teachers sketch a composite picture of multiple ways teachers can plan to link what their students need to know to purposeful arts-infused lesson activities.

Before we examine some theory, rationale, and terminology related to purposeful planning, *remember that this book is designed to help you plan and implement successful arts activities across your own classroom or future classroom curriculum.* As such, this book both is a self-study in curriculum development (Posner, 1995; Wiggins & McTighe, 2006) and contains suggestions for reflective experiences with others (if discussion suggestions are used in methods classes, online, or with practicing peers at school sites).

Theory and Rationale: Reflective Practices and Constructive Curriculum Planning

This chapter was organized to have you first consider the ideas of practicing K–8 classroom teachers engaged in the initial construction of their own lesson ideas. In other words, their examples helped construct your awareness, just as your own teaching constructs or will construct your knowledge of teaching and learning.

Through your reading, you have become a reflective practitioner along with our teacher contributors (Schon, 1983, 1987, 1991). You did not read complete lessons in this chapter, rather the initial, mindful constructs and reflections of teachers who seek to use the arts to help teach what their students need to know. What you read were the beginnings of our teacher contributors' curriculum mapping (Wiggins & McTighe, 2006).

Chapter 2 did not begin with what Posner (1995) calls "top-down," systematic prescriptions or examples of formulated teaching sequences everyone should use to infuse the arts into content curriculum. (Perhaps this may be a disappointment for some readers, as prescriptions can provide a secure structure. However, they may or may not be effectively tied to what our own students need to know.) Instead, you were immediately immersed in narratives of how real teachers plan to use real ideas (Sagor, 1993; Stringer, 1999).

Through your reading experience, you may have begun to construct your own thoughts, similarly beginning to think about and address the needs of your own students. In other words, the construction of your own future lessons has undoubtedly already begun.

What Students Need to Know: Key Ideas Toward Student Understanding

What follows is a series of key ideas from research related to the content of this chapter:

Careful Choices

In this initial stage of your purposeful planning, you are to consider your content goals, examining various grade-appropriate content standards as you consider your own classroom or future classroom curriculum expectations. According to Wiggins and McTighe (2006), we must make careful choices in our first stages of planning and establish "clarity about priorities" (p. 18).

Backward Curriculum Design

This chapter's focus, "what our students need to know," implies what Wiggins and McTighe (2006) pinpoint as a desired, "backward" design in curriculum planning. In other words, *the focus is on student learning*, a results-focus design based on desired student output linked to various forms of assessment.

> To put it in an odd way, too many teachers focus on the *teaching* and not the *learning*. They spend most of their time thinking, first, about what they will do, what materials they will use, and what they will ask students to do rather than first considering what the learner will need in order to accomplish the learning goal" (Wiggins & McTighe, 2006, p. 15).

Education for Understanding

Additional considerations for what your students need to know become, "What content is worthy of understanding? What enduring understandings are desired?" (Wiggins & McTighe, 2006, p. 17).

Big ideas. Big ideas are a focus of education for understanding. According to Wiggins and McTighe (2006), "A big idea is a concept, theme, or issue that gives meaning and connection to discrete facts and skills." (p. 5)

What students should know and be able to do. What students should know and be able to do (or desired results) may be intended outcomes, achievement targets, or performance standards. "All four terms are meant to shift our focus away from the inputs to the output: what the student should be able to know, do and understand upon leaving, expressed in performance and product terms" (Wiggins & McTighe, 2006, p. 6).

What we want our students to understand. What we want our students to understand has layers of meaning.

> To *understand* is to make connections and bind together our knowledge into something that makes sense of things (whereas without understanding we might see only unclear, isolate, or unhelpful facts). But the word also implies doing, not just a mental act. . . . To understand is to be able to wisely and effective *use*—transfer—what we know, in context; to *apply* knowledge and skill effectively, in realistic tasks and settings. To have understood means that we show evidence of being able to transfer what we know. When we understand, we have a fluent and fluid grasp, not a rigid, formulaic grasp based only on recall and "plugging in." (Wiggins & McTighe, 2006, p. 7).

Reflective Practices: The Importance of Others in Your Planning

Practicing professionals work within a domain of common language about problems known only to peers within the same practice. When they converse as they plan and problem solve, their constructive dialogue can result in a change of knowing (Cranton, 1994, 1996; Doyle, 1990; Mezirow, 1990, 1991, 1997; Schon, 1983, 1987, 1991).

Professionals and pre-professionals need others in order to learn, change, and grow. There is purpose in their conversations. Peers can help other others reframe and rethink teaching challenges. Through thoughtful construction and critical reframing of the needs and problems in one's teaching practice, experimentation and discovery of new methods may emerge from interaction with others (McDonald, 2000).

Cranton (1996) comments on the role of critical reflection toward transforming adult practice by stating, "Critical reflection is the key to learning from experience. Educators learn about teaching by talking about their experiences, becoming aware of the assumptions and expectations they have, questioning these assumptions, and possibly revising their perspectives" (p. 2).

Professional, constructive dialogues require good listening skills, or what Meier (1996) terms actions of "informed empathy . . . a willingness to suspend belief long enough to entertain ideas contrary to our own, and the expectation that our ideas are forever in progress, unfinished, and incomplete. . . . Learning empathy is not a 'soft' subject; it is the hardest one of all. It must marry imagination and scholarship" (p. 272). With these considerations in mind, discuss your ideas with and for others as you listen well.

2.5 Discuss, Write, Discuss Again

Discuss and then fill in your self-study, Figure 2.1: You may find it helpful to participate in the structured discussion (outlined below) with a method class or school-site peer *before* you fill out your self-study responses in Figure 2.1, "What Students Need to Know." Then, after you have completed the self-study, discuss and exchange your written ideas with another peer or small group of peers.

Interaction with Peers

Before you are guided through this book's first purposeful planning self-study exercise, let's first consider some suggestions for discussion. These prompts may provide rich opportunities for you to initially think about and discuss your ideas as you learn from peers in your methods class, at school-sites, and through possible online or phone conversations. The question prompts could also be used in informal dialogues with peers at your school site.

Suggestions for Discussion Topics

- What "big ideas" in our curriculum do our students need to know and be able to do? Why?
- Which of these needs seem to lend themselves to arts inclusion linked to content area instruction? Why?
- Which arts should we seek to include? Why?
- What are some ways we think we might use/link arts activities within a selected lesson? List.
- How do we imagine that these kinds of arts activities might enrich teaching and student learning based on what students need to know? How? Why?
- By the end of an imagined lesson using the arts within a content lesson, what will students be able to know and do?
- Finally, what do we hope to accomplish or have happen during this lesson?

Conclusion

In this chapter, you have considered many excellent initial planning models from our teacher-contributors. You have consequently begun to construct your own purposeful planning based on what students need to know and be able to do across the classroom curriculum.

Self-Study

What Students Need to Know

In this Self-Study you will be guided through the same constructive planning processes as our contributing K–8 classroom teachers.

Here are some suggestions for using Figure 2.1, "Self-Study: What Students Need to Know" (p. 54):

- First, discuss your ideas with others (see list of suggestions for discussion in previous section)
- Second, fill in Figure 2.1, "What Students Need to Know."
- Third, share your ideas: Self-study responses may be easily shared with others electronically. The contents of this form (Figure 2.1) can also be used in further methods class or school-site discussions.
- Then start a file of arts-infused lesson ideas. Save your own version of this form in your computer files as the beginning of your integrated lesson file. You may also wish to create and save hard copies of the form to share in class discussions and/or include in a hard copy, integrated lesson file.

FIGURE 2.1 Self-Study: What Students Need to Know

Purposeful Planning

Name: _____ Date: _____ Grade or Subject: _____

School Site/ Methods Class: _____

Topic or Lesson Theme: _____

Content Area(s): _____

Art or arts you would like to use: _____ _____ _____ _____

Why did you pick this instructional theme or focus? (2 or 3 sentences)

What are some of the *big ideas* your students need to know within this content area theme?
(Write an abbreviated list with 3–7 "big ideas" or concepts)

List content area standards involving these "big ideas":

By the end of this integrated arts unit about _____, my students will know and be able to do (what?).

How do you think or hope the arts activities (music, dance, theatre, visual art) infusion might enrich your instruction and learning within this curriculum or content theme? Why? (2 or 3 sentences)

What I *hope to accomplish* in this integrated lesson (a paragraph (4–6 sentences) describing ideas and events in this lesson—continue on the back of the page, if needed)

References

Carle, E. (1994). *The very hungry caterpillar.* New York: Philomel.

Covey, S. (1989). *The seven habits of highly effective people: Powerful lessons in personal change.* New York: Free Press.

Cranton, P. (1996). *Professional development as transformative learning: New perspectives for teachers of adults.* San Francisco: Jossey-Bass.

Doyle, W. (1990). Case methods in the education of teachers. *Teacher Education Quarterly, 17,* 7–15.

McDonald, N. (2000). Constructivist listening: Real life discipline and management concerns. *General Music Today 13*(2), 3–7.

Meier, D. (1996). Supposing that. *Phi Delta Kappan, 78*(4), 271–276.

Mezirow, J. (1990). *Fostering critical reflection in adulthood: A guide to transformative and emancipatory learning.* San Francisco: Jossey-Bass.

Mezirow, J. (1991). *Transformative dimensions of adult learning.* San Francisco: Jossey-Bass.

Mezirow, J. (1997). Transformative learning: Theory to practice. *New Directions for Adult and Continuing Education, 74,* 5–12.

Posner, G. (1995). *Analyzing the curriculum* (2nd ed.). New York: McGraw-Hill.

Sagor, R. (1993). *How to conduct collaborative action research.* Alexandria, VA: Association for Supervision and Curriculum Development.

Schecter, D. (1997). *Science Art: Projects and Activities that Teach Science Concepts and Develop Process Skills.* New York: Scholastic.

Schon, D. (1983). *The reflective practitioner: How professionals think in action.* New York: Harper Collins.

Schon, D. (1987). *Educating the reflective practitioner: Toward a new design for teaching and learning in the professions.* San Francisco: Jossey-Bass.

Schon, D. (1991). *The reflective turn: Case studies in and on educational practices.* New York: Teachers College Press.

Stringer, R. (1999). *Action research* (2nd ed.). Thousand Oaks, CA: Sage.

Wiggins, G., & McTighe, J. (2006). *Understanding by design handbook* (2nd ed.). Alexandria, VA: Association for Supervision and Curriculum Development.

chapter 3

What Students Already Know

Man can learn nothing except by going from the known to the unknown.

—Claude Bernard

FOCUS ACTIVITY

Directions: Please fill out before and after reading this chapter.

Before Reading Chapter A = agree D = disagree	Statements	After Reading Chapter A = agree D = disagree
	I need to know what students already know about a topic *before* planning my instruction.	
	I know of multiple ways to easily find out what students already know about a topic before instruction begins.	
	Knowledge is "understanding."	
	I can imagine ways in which arts activities could help fill the gap between what students already know and what they need to know about a chosen topic.	

This chapter will focus on uncovering what your students already know about a topic and how that information can shape your own purposeful planning with the arts. The gap between what students *already know* and what they *need to know* will be addressed as well as how arts activities and engagement can be purposely planned to help close this gap in student understanding. Further opportunities for self-study and peer discussion appear at the end of this chapter.

What Students Already Know

It is likely that all of us acknowledge the importance of knowing what our students already know before we begin any type of classroom instruction. You may have or will soon formulate multiple ways of assessing previous knowledge on a day-by-day basis (by observation, written assessments and surveys, discussions, checklists, etc.) Most teachers do.

However, this book is concerned with your own purposeful planning with the arts across the curriculum. Toward that goal, it might be helpful to consider how some of our teacher contributors found out what their students already knew and used that information to guide their arts-infused lesson planning.

Let's revisit a few lessons from our teacher contributors.

● IN THE CLASSROOM

Integrating Social Studies/History and the Arts: "Jamestown in 1607" Content Areas: History/Social Science, English Language Arts (Writing and Speaking), Arts (Theatre)

Previously, you read about Mrs. Crandall's fifth-grade social studies/language arts/theatre lesson, "Jamestown in 1607." In her planning for this lesson, Mrs. Crandall wanted to infuse her students' study of Jamestown with point-of-view emphasis in writing and performing a dramatic reenactment. In order "to gain insight into what life was like in Jamestown, I want students to research and reenact a person's life from that time period to 'feel' what it was like to live back then."

● l e s s o n   t r a c k e r   r e p l a y

Mrs. Crandall's "Jamestown in 1607"

Big Ideas

Mrs. Crandall's "big ideas" her students need to know and "do" in **Social Studies** are:

- Jobs colonists worked on in Jamestown
- Colonists had to work hard in the new colony to survive and thrive
- Research and study the various jobs people had and reenact the colonists' jobs for their peers.

She plans to infuse the art of **Theatre** into her lesson by using (Notice the language arts, reading, and speaking skills involved in theatre.):

- Script writing and acting linked to characters within what they learned about authentic historical periods and settings
- Characterization through writing from a historical person's perspective and voice
- Acting and performing, analyzing performances for and by peers

When asked how she found out what her students already knew about Jamestown, Mrs. Crandall offered the following:

I knew the students had studied the Pilgrims within previous grade's social studies content. Most students know something about the Pilgrims, but little if anything about Jamestown.

When beginning a new topic, I create a chart on an overhead transparency. I use a K-W-L chart format (Ogle, 1986) with three column categories, "What Do We Know?" "What Do We Want to Know?" and "What Have We Learned?"

3.1 K-W-L

For more about K-W-L technique and the modified versions of K-W-L, see the following sources:

Carr, E., & Ogle, D. (1987). K-W-L plus: A strategy for comprehension and summarization. *Journal of Reading, 30*, 626–631.

Ogle, D. (1986). K-W-L: A teaching model that develops active reading of expository text. *The Reading Teacher, 39*, 564–570.

Schmidt, P. R. (1999). KWLQ: Inquiry and literacy learning in science. *The Reading Teacher, 52*, 789–792.

3.2 Resource for Text to World Connections

For more about text to world connections see:

Keene, E. O., & Zimmermann, S. (1997). *Mosaic of thought: Teaching comprehension in a reader's workshop.* Portsmouth, NH: Heinemann.

I first ask the students what they know about Jamestown. There is usually very little response. So, I prompt them by asking probing questions, "Do you think Jamestown is a place?" "Where is it?" "Who do you think lived there?" etc. I list all ideas, even if they are guesses or misconceptions, and they frequently are.

After those initial questions, I make a text to world connection (Keene & Zimmermann, 1997) by asking, "Has anyone seen the film *Pocahontas?*" Many hands go up. Once I tell the students that this film was set in Jamestown, light bulbs go off!

My students begin to connect to what they know about Jamestown through what they remembered about the movie. Many more hands go up and I list those ideas. What they know about Jamestown from viewing the film usually has to do with the names of the characters, Pocahontas and Captain John Smith, and what happened during the film story. Some students try to identify the time period and approximate where Jamestown might be.

From there I go to the next K-W-L category, "What Do We Want to Know?" I say, "Based on what you know, what do you want to find out more about concerning Jamestown in 1607?" I invite my students to partner talk to formulate and write out questions they are interested in answering. Examples include, "What buildings were there?" "What did people do there?" "Where did the natives live?" "What were some problems they had?" I write out all student questions on the overhead.

FIGURE 3.1 K-W-L Chart (Ogle, 1986) Used by Mrs. Crandall

What Do We Know?	What Do We Want to Know?	What Have We Learned?

These and other questions become the platform for my student's inquiry into Jamestown. After the entire lesson is completed, we will fill in the last column "What Have We Learned?" together. There, we can all see how we answered our own questions.

● BEYOND THE CLASSROOM ....

Stay current with what students are seeing, hearing, and reading: Think about the many forms of media students experience during their daily lives (television, cartoons, internet, video games, music CDs, current events news programs, newspapers, films, magazines, books, etc.). These common experiences can provide your students with important connections to new information. To find out more about these common experiences, ask students to write about or discuss a favorite TV show, an interesting news event, video game, music CD, or film. Importantly, once you've got a list of their interests, experience the media yourself.

Anticipatory Activities as Platforms for Inquiry

Mrs. Crandall wanted to find out what her students already knew about Jamestown. In addition, her intent was to start her lesson with *anticipatory activities designed to grab her student's attention.* Frey and Fisher (2007) add insight to this technique by stating,

> When we speak of attention, we are not referring to behavior management, but rather to practices that elicit curiosity, provoke questions, and evoke recall of newly learned information. In addition, attention means activating students' background knowledge about the topic. This is really the very beginning of the learning process, although it is not bound in time to the beginning of a course, class, or lesson. Good and Brophy (2002) remind us that effective teachers create memorable events throughout their lessons to capture student attention. (p. 46)

At the beginning of her lesson, Mrs. Crandall initiated a class discussion using K-W-L technique and text-to-world connections to uncover and list what her students already knew about Jamestown. Through her anticipatory activities, Mrs. Crandall asked thought-provoking questions. By doing so she invited her students to formulate their own

3.3 Resource in Reading Instruction

For more research-based, classroom-proven strategies to develop strong skills for student success in reading for information see:

Frey, N., & Fisher, D. (2007). *Reading for information in elementary school: Content literacy strategies to build comprehension.* Upper Saddle River, NJ: Merrill/Prentice Hall.

questions to develop further understanding of the topic at hand (Brandt, 1992; Muncy, Payne, & White, 1999).

In other words, she and her students established a *platform for inquiry* for their upcoming projects (theatre: historical reenactments). The questions the students created in partner sharing became the organizational structure of their reading, research, script writing, and historical reenactments of Jamestown in 1607. In this way, the students' background knowledge and curiosity actively helped scaffold the lesson.

Frey and Fisher (2007) further comment,

> It is essential to note that gaining attention through anticipatory activities is not intended to provide entertainment for students, but rather to scaffold learning so that the responsibility for learning shifts to the student. A primary goal of classroom instruction is to move from teacher-directed instruction to student-centered learning. Anticipatory activities can ground new learning in meaning-based inquiry, because the students' attention is gained through an event that is connected to the purpose for studying the topic. (p. 46)

lesson tracker

Mrs. Crandall's "Jamestown in 1607"

Techniques to Find Out What Students Already Know
Mrs. Crandall used the following techniques:

- Anticipatory activity: Class discussion.
- Thought-provoking questions about the topic.
- K-W-L chart on overhead—elicited student input.
- Text-to-World connections (popular film).
- Students work individually or in pairs to formulate written questions about "What Do We Want to Know?" Share with class and list on K-W-L chart.
- Student questions become *platform of inquiry* for their integrated, project-based lesson.

Mrs. Crandall chose to infuse the art of theatre (script writing and historical character reenactment) as the *expressive avenue or context for students to connect what they already knew to what they read and learned.* They were to "show" what they learned. As such, the students were challenged to create scripts and performances to *connect and make meaning* (for themselves and the whole class audience) of the historical facts about life in Jamestown, 1607.

● IN THE CLASSROOM

"Orchid Paragraphs" Content Areas: Language Arts/Literacy, Arts (Visual Art, Music)

In the beginning of this book, you read about Mrs. Laws's second-grade Language Arts/
Literacy and Visual Art lesson "Orchid Paragraphs." Her idea was to invite a guest artist (her
father) to demonstrate pastel chalk sketching of an orchid still-life model; discuss/apply new
visual art vocabulary and techniques with the students (ELL and special learner accommodations included); lead her students in their own sketches; and then discuss, write, and peer
edit narrative/reflective paragraphs about their common experiences.

● l e s s o n   t r a c k e r   r e p l a y

Mrs. Law's "Orchid Paragraphs"
Big Ideas

● Students need to develop and use new vocabulary in writing (brief narratives) and speaking
based on a common, direct experience in visual arts.

● Visual arts activity can generate new vocabulary and interest in writing and speaking about
that hands-on activity.

When asked how she found out what her students already knew about writing paragraphs, Mrs. Laws comments,

My students are lower level English Language Learners at the intermediate and early
intermediate levels. When I ask students to construct paragraphs, it is typical that the
students might mention going to the movies. Then the next sentence might jump to
what they had for dinner last night. Due to their limited and developing English skills,
their writing often lacks point of reference, flow, sequence, and vocabulary.

Mrs. Laws adds,

A teacher should *always* know where the kids are
in their skills. I do this by constantly listening to how
they speak and how they discuss topics with their
peers, reading how they write, and observing how
they draw and discuss their work, etc. It's an ongoing
process.

When asked what her students already knew about
visual art, Mrs. Laws knew they had had some successful

3.4 **Resources in Visual Art**

For more about information and resources for
using *visual art techniques and projects* during
content instruction see Appendix: Resource
Bibliography.

class experience with sketching (and loved it) and had also worked with watercolor media. She knew her students had never worked with chalk pastels and were ready to increase their knowledge, English language vocabulary, and experience within a new medium. She knew (from past experience) her students would be very excited about watching a guest artist use this new medium and would want to try techniques on their own.

Mrs. Laws used what she knew about her students' interest in visual art to create opportunities for a

common experience where my students would all experience the same thing at the same time, and in the same order. My students would all watch the artist's model, hear and respond to his questions, learn new vocabulary in application to his art processes, etc. They could then "do" their own artwork (guided process led by the artist) incorporating the vocabulary and techniques they learned using a new medium (pastel chalk). Because they had this common, hands-on point of reference, my students could then discuss and write about what the artist did and said, what they actually did in their own artwork, etc.

My students would be able to help each other in the sequence and content of their writing (peer editing), as the experiences were known and experienced by all.

● l e s s o n   t r a c k e r

"Orchid Paragraphs" Techniques to Find Out What Students Already Know

Mrs. Laws used the following techniques:

- (Ongoing) assessment of student paragraph writing used to determine her students were lacking flow, sequence, point of reference, and vocabulary
- (Ongoing) assessment of her student's abilities in visual art activities used to determine that they already knew how to sketch and were always excited when they learned about new art media, vocabulary, process, and techniques. Mrs. Laws used determined her students would welcome learning new ideas from a guest artist.
- Anticipatory activity: Classroom demonstration
- Artist demonstration of sketching, art vocabulary, and new media
- Artist Q & A with students, guided independent sketches
- Discussion, paragraph writing, peer editing

Experiential Learning: The Role of Direct Experience in Lesson Scaffolding

Mrs. Laws did an interesting thing. Through listening, reading, and observing her students as they spoke, wrote, and sketched, she thought of a creative, arts-infused lesson to cover a lot of instructional territory. Furthermore, out of her knowledge about what her students already knew, she was able to *formulate an interesting common experience as a point of reference used to improve her student's writing.*

In the anticipatory activities for this lesson, Mrs. Laws incorporated a live classroom demonstration of visual art techniques and vocabulary. The guest artist was able to display concepts and integrate sequence, process, and vocabulary into his live demonstration. According to Frey and Fisher (2007),

> Many educators acknowledge the role of experience in learning (Dewey, 1938). The transformative nature of experiences can assist learners in connecting knowledge to its application and variation in the larger world. Experiences can also provoke reflection as students begin to understand that knowledge is not fixed, but is constantly tested by new experiences (Kolb, 1984). This theory, called experiential learning, has its roots in the work of John Dewey and has been extended by brain-based research of the past decade.

Importantly, during the artist demonstration, students in Mrs. Laws's class knew they needed to *pay attention and remember what happened and why* (they would soon be using pastels to sketch their own orchid still life). The demonstration and independent art activity were thus designed to help *scaffold* student writing activities as the students wrote about what happened, what they did, and learned. Peer editing was aided by common experiences where students could help other students correctly use new vocabulary and create a more meaningful reflection of their visual art experience.

The students in Mrs. Laws's class were able to learn new vocabulary and visual art techniques from the guest artist within the context of viewing his process. They were then able to directly *apply* that learning within *personalized, active, and expressive contexts* (their individual sketches, paragraphs, and discussions). *Visual art activity was therefore an important catalyst for accessing student's memory of the learning at hand and their ability to retrieve and apply information learned* (McDonald & Fisher, 2006).

Through visual arts activity, Mrs. Laws's students' language was developed through multiple stimuli, both verbal and nonverbal. To this, McDonald and Fisher (2002) comment,

> Vygotsky (1978) argued that human language is developed through multiple signals, both verbal and nonverbal, during which learners connect learning to what they already know. Synthesis takes place through a child's active involvement with the meanings of language. Furthermore, we know the centrality of human language toward thinking and that a child's learning depends on language, cutting across learning within all subject matter and school activity. (p. 16).

Experiential Learning: The Role of Direct Experience in Lesson Scaffolding

Mrs. Laws's students were able to process stimuli within the guest artist's demonstration and then actively connect to their existing knowledge about how to sketch and write. *Through the careful and purposeful scaffolding of her lesson based on what her students already knew, Mrs. Laws was able to incorporate important and creative opportunities to increase student learning.*

Let's consider a few more techniques for finding out what our students already know about a topic at hand.

Tools for Finding Out What Students Already Know

What follows is a short list of suggested activities and techniques for finding out what students already know. (While many of these activities are traditionally used at the beginning of a lesson experience, they may also be used throughout a lesson to inform you about what your students know.)

Thought-Provoking Questions (K-W-L)

Pose questions to students that *cannot be simply answered* (Frey & Fisher, 2007). Do so to prompt them to think about what they know and what they want to learn. These types of questions promote student curiosity and invite students to develop their own understanding of the material (Brandt, 1992; Muncy, Payne, & White, 1999).

The K-W-L (Ogle, 1986) example you read in Mrs. Crandall's Jamestown lesson uses a sequenced structure of provocative questions (What Do We Know? What Do We Want to Know? What Have We Learned??) to guide classroom discussion, list student ideas, and structure student inquiry.

Over the years, the K-W-L technique has been augmented to include K-W-L Plus (Carr & Ogle, 1987). Summarization is added. K-W-L-H (Wills, 1995) adds another column category, "*How* do I know?" with a final focus on the sources of student information or evidence. Discussion in this category may serve you well in finding out more about how your students learn and retain information. K-W-L-Q (Schmidt, 1999) adds yet another category for *further questions* the students may have at the *end* of the lesson or unit. These questions could provide important insight into what your students want to learn in the future.

Visual Displays

Hyerle (1996) refers to the use of visual tools for constructing knowledge. Just like other forms of literacy (reading, writing, speaking, and listening), the viewing of visual displays is acknowledged as an essential element of communication (Flood, Heath, & Lapp, 1997). As you know, your students are accustomed to a rapid plethora of visual stimuli and are quite adept at processing multiple visual images (Jensen, 2005). More and more teachers are tapping into how their students naturally construct knowledge from computers, CD-ROMs, web-based resources, and other digital technologies. These types of media-based activities are interactive and illicit "active participation of the learner" (Frey & Fisher, 2007, p. 49).

Technology Assisted Visual Displays:

- *Use video clips to "set the scene" for learning:* Ask students what they know about the topic based on what they saw and heard.
- *Visit website information related to the topic at hand:* Project information for whole class viewing. Ask students K-W-L questions based on this online information.
- *Project items from online museum collections found at their websites:* Use appropriate paintings, photography, graphic designs, sculpture, architecture, folk crafts, etc. in classroom discussion.
- *Project visual images:* Use images from student textbooks, library books, and other informational sources as prompts for inquiry.
- *Project photographs and text:* Use images and text from newspapers, magazines, comics, etc., to illicit classroom discussion about the topic at hand.
- *Project digital photos of past students engaged in the lesson activities your current students are about to do:* Ask the students what they think the past students are doing and learning.

BEYOND THE CLASSROOM

Many museum websites have fabulous online collections available for classroom projection. Contact your local museums (art, natural history, science, history, photographic arts) for educational materials and resources. Visit the following and other museum websites for online resources and lesson plan materials:

Louvre Museum: www.louvre.fr

Metropolitan Museum of Art: www.metmuseum.org.

Smithsonian: www.smithsonianeducation.org. Take some time for students to search online for other museum collections and make a list of the visual art they found related to a topic of interest.

Quick Writes

Quick writes can be used in introductory lesson activities to uncover previous knowledge and personal experiences. Teachers can easily initiate quick, timed, written student responses to thought-provoking questions to "activate background knowledge and personal experience" (Frey & Fisher, 2007, pp. 50–51). Students enjoy the brevity of these experiences as well as the contrast to other, more formal classroom writing experiences. Daniels and Bizar (1998) describe the differences between quick writes and other process pieces in the following way:

- spontaneous vs. planned
- short vs. lengthy
- exploratory vs. authoritative
- expressive vs. transactional
- informal vs. formal
- personal vs. audience-centered
- unedited vs. polished
- ungraded vs. graded

(p. 114, as quoted in Frey & Fisher, 2007, p. 51)

Examples of Quick Write Prompts

- Simply ask students to "write about what they know" about a topic (e.g., "What do you know about spiders?"). Encourage them to include their personal experiences with that information.
- After showing a visual image or reading a written passage about a topic at hand, ask students to write their short responses to that experience. Ask students to describe what they thought, felt, already know, or think about the experience. Tap into student written responses within group discussions.

Anticipation Guides

An anticipation guide creates a record of what students know (and believe) before and then after new information and lesson experiences (see Figure 3.2). They usually feature clearly written true-or-false statements to assess what the learner knows and does not know, both before and after the lesson. They are easy to use, are not graded, and are simply used to inform you (the teacher) of students' background knowledge. (In this book, anticipation guides appear in the "Focus Activity" at the beginning of each chapter.)

FIGURE 3.2 Anticipation Guide for Fifth-Grade Social Studies

Name: _____   Date: _____

Anticipation Guide—What Do You Know About the American Revolution?

Directions: Read each statement and put a "+" in the Before column for true statements and a "O" for false statements. You will answer again at the end of this unit.

Before Lesson	Is this statement true or false?	After Lesson
	1. The British helped the first settlers protect themselves from some Native American tribes.	
	2. The Stamp Act was a law about collecting stamps.	
	3. Angry colonists dumped 342 crates of tea into Boston Harbor in an event called the Boston Tea Party.	
	4. Loyalists wanted to become independent from England.	
	5. Patriots wanted to be Americans and not citizens of England.	
	6. During the American Revolution, everyone chose a side.	
	7. There were 14 colonies involved in the American Revolution.	
	8. The Declaration of Independence made the colonies free from British rule.	

Source: From *Reading for information in elementary school: Content literacy strategies to build comprehension.* (p. 65, Figure 3.7), by N. Frey and D. Fisher 2007, Upper Saddle River, NJ: Merrill/Prentice Hall. Reprinted with permission.

Demonstrations

By now, you have read a great deal about the guest artist demonstration in Mrs. Laws's "Orchid Paragraphs" lesson. Demonstrations and guest speakers (both live and through media) are a highly effective tool to engage student interest and connect learning within a context of a common experience—*a real event.*

Examples of Other Guest Speakers and Demonstrations

- *Social Studies:* Invited guests with origins in other countries share stories, tales, songs, language, clothing, photographs, arts and crafts, food, history, customs, and memories of their country. Create a flyer asking parents, grandparents, and other family members to visit your present or future classroom.
- *Science:* Invited guests share their area of expertise within a live demonstration in your classroom (chemist, entomologist, weather expert, computer expert, graphic arts engineer, etc.)
- *Music and Dance:* Invited college students, parents, or community members play their instruments and/or sing or dance. These artists could share information about their instruments, training, and art form.
- *Theatre/Social Studies/History:* Invited performers reenact historically based monologues, dialogues, or scenes as characters in period costumes.

Learning With Understanding: Arts Activity and Transfer of Student Knowledge

In addition to knowledge and skill about a set of facts and/or procedures and events concerning an instructional topic, you also want your students *to understand* what they have learned. *Understanding* implies transfer or application to new situations and contexts, a broader sense of making meaning of what is learned (Wiggins & McTighe, 2006). Additionally,

> The ability to transfer our knowledge and skill effectively involves the capacity to take what we know and use it creatively, flexibly, fluently, in different settings or problems, on our own. Transferability is not mere plugging in of previously learned knowledge and skill. Understanding is about "going beyond the information given." We can create new knowledge and arrive at further understandings if we have learned with understanding some key ideas and strategies." (Wiggins & McTighe, 2006, p. 40)

As you read earlier in both Mrs. Laws's and Mrs. Crandall's lessons (and in the many contributing teachers' lessons you have read, arts activities can be purposely infused within content area instruction in order to provide opportunities for students to apply and connect what they learned and already knew to new situations within new contexts. By doing so in both verbal and nonverbal ways, students are able to connect and actively make meaning of what they learned in new and exciting ways. Wiggins and McTighe (2006) add,

Developing the ability to transfer one's learning is key to a good education (Bransford, Brown, & Cocking, 2000). It is an essential ability because teachers can only help students learn a relatively small number of ideas, examples, facts, and skills in the entire field of study; so we need to help them transfer their inherently limited learning to many other settings, issues, and problems. (p. 40)

Additionally, the arts can provide important new settings, contexts, and expressive avenues for students to bridge the gap between what they already know and what they need to know.

Conclusion

In this chapter, you considered the importance of finding out what your students already know about a topic of study, ways to effectively illicit that information, and how that information can be used to shape arts-infused lesson planning and activities. You read how the arts can provide creative and effective contexts to increase student understanding—the transfer and application of knowledge, facts, and skills into meaningful and memorable new contexts—thereby helping to bridge the gap between what students already know and what they need to know.

Self-Study

What Students Already Know

Let's now consider how the arts might be incorporated to help bridge the gap between what your students already know and what they need to know about your chosen topic. Now that you have read many examples of how to find out what students already know about a topic, let's turn our attention back to the arts-infused lesson idea(s) you have been purposefully planning. First, glance again at your work on the self-study at the end of Chapter 2 (Figure 2.1, "Self-Study: What the Students Need to Know).

How to Complete the Self-Study

What follows are helpful suggestions for how to complete this chapter's self-study:

- *Refer* to your self-study form, "Self-Study: What Students Need to Know," from the end of Chapter 2. (IMPORTANT NOTE: Keep working on the same lesson idea to be developed throughout this book's self-study exercises.)

- *Confer* with a peer partner or small group. Each person can briefly share their ideas from Chapter 2's self-study.
- *Fill in the new form* for this chapter, Figure 3.3, "Self-Study: What Students Already Know," which follows. Take your time in this reflection. *Remember to use the same lesson idea you began in Chapter 2.*
- *Discuss* your ideas from this new self-study (Figure 3.3) with a methods class peer (or school-site peer) or small group, and revise and/or add ideas as appropriate.
- *Share your ideas:* Your answers on this self-study can be shared electronically with peers and used in further methods class or school-site discussions.
- *Continue to create your file of arts-infused lesson ideas:* Save this form in your computer files as the next component of your customized arts-infused lesson file. You may also wish to make and save hard copies of the form to share in class discussions and/or include in a hard copy, arts-infused lesson file.

References

Brandt, R. (1992). On Deming and school quality: A conversation with Enid Brown. *Educational Leadership, 50*(3), 28–31.

Bransford, J., Brown, A., & Cocking, R. (Eds.). (2000). *How people learn: Brain, mind, experience, and school.* Washington, DC: National Research Council.

Bruner, J. (1973). *Beyond the information given: Studies in the psychology of knowing.* New York: W. W. Norton. (Original work published 1923)

Carr, E., & Ogle, D. (1987). K-W-L plus: A strategy for comprehension and summarization, *Journal of Reading, 30,* 626–631.

Daniels, H., & Bizar, M. (1998). *Methods that matter: Six structures for best practice classrooms.* York, ME: Stenhouse.

Dewey, J. (1938). *Experience and education.* New York: Macmillan.

Flood, D., Heath, S., & Lapp, D. (1997). *Research on teaching literacy through the communicative and visual arts.* Newark, DE: International Reading Association.

Frey, N., & Fisher, D. (2007). *Reading for information in elementary school: Content literacy strategies to build comprehension.* Upper Saddle River, NJ: Merrill/Prentice Hall.

Good, T., & Brophy, J. (2002). *Looking in classrooms* (9th ed.). New York: Harper Collins.

Hyerle, D. (1996). *Visual tools for constructing knowledge.* Alexandria, VA: Association of Supervision and Curriculum Development.

Jensen, E. (2005). *Teaching with the brain in mind* (2nd ed.). Alexandria, VA: Association for Supervision and Curriculum Development.

Keene, E. O., & Zimmermann, S. (1997). *Mosaic of thought: Teaching comprehension in a reader's workshop.* Portsmouth, NH: Heinemann.

Kolb, D. (1984). *Experiential learning: Experience as the source of learning and development.* Englewood Cliffs, NJ: Prentice Hall.

McDonald, N., & Fisher, D. (2002). *Developing arts-loving readers: Top ten questions teachers are asking about integrated arts education.* Lanham, MD: Rowman & Littlefield Education.

Figure 3.3 Self-Study: "What Students Already Know"

Purposeful Planning

(IMPORTANT NOTE: Continue to work on the same lesson idea you began in Chapter 2 of this book.)

Name: _____ Date: _____ Grade/Subject: _____

School Site/ Methods Class: _____

Topic or Lesson Theme: _____

Content Area(s): _____

Art or arts you would like to use:_____ _____ _____ _____

Once again, *why* did you pick this instructional theme or focus? (2 or 3 sentences)

What do you *think* students might already know about this topic? *How* do they know these things?
(make a bulleted list, explain)

What are some *misconceptions* you think students might have about this topic? Why? (list and explain)

***How* can you find out what the students already know about this topic? List ways you could find out what students already know.**

Refer to your filled-out Chapter 2 "Self-Study Form: What Students Need to Know."

Once you find out what students already know, how will this affect your ideas for your lesson?

How do you think the arts activities you have selected for your lesson might help *bridge the gap between student's previous knowledge and what they need to know?* Why?

List some *major understandings* you *hope* your students will gain about your topic through their arts activities experiences.

McDonald, N., & Fisher, D. (2006). *Teaching literacy through the arts.* New York: Guilford.

Muncy, D., Payne, J., & White, N. (1999). Making curriculum and instructional reform happen: A case study. *Peabody Journal of Education, 74,* 68–110.

Ogle, D. (1986). K-W-L: A teaching model that develops active reading of expository text. *The Reading Teacher, 39,* 564–570.

Schmidt, P. R. (1999). KWLQ: Inquiry and literacy learning in science. *The Reading Teacher, 52,* 789–792.

Vygotsky, L. (1978). *Mind in society: The development of higher mental psychological processes.* Cambridge, MA: Harvard University Press.

Wiggins, G., & McTighe, J. (2006). *Understanding by design handbook* (2nd ed.). Alexandria, VA: Association for Supervision and Curriculum Development

Wills, C. (1995). Voice of inquiry: Possibilities and perspectives. *Childhood Education, 71,* 261–265.

Selecting Resources

Trust that still, small voice that says, "This might work and I'll try it."

—Diane Mariechild

FOCUS ACTIVITY

Directions: Please fill out before and after reading this chapter.

Before Reading Chapter A = agree D = disagree	Statements	After Reading Chapter A = agree D = disagree
	I can imagine a variety of ways in which arts materials and activities could be used in my teaching.	
	One or more of the arts are within my "comfort zone" for teaching.	
	I do not have time or expertise to look for arts-infused lesson materials.	
	I already use or know how to use a number of arts resources and materials in content teaching.	
	I have a set of criteria to locate and select appropriate arts-infused lesson materials within content teaching.	
	Integrated arts resources are interesting but most are not helpful to me.	
	Resources need to show me how to use those arts materials in a prescribed teaching sequence.	
	Arts-related materials (appropriate for classroom teacher use) are available at my university, school site, district, and surrounding community.	

The focus in this chapter is to explore, locate, and select appropriate materials matched to your own arts-infused teaching goals and student needs. You will use a personalized *materials criteria checklist* as you search for and select appropriate resources for your arts-infused lesson(s). (Note: A wide range of resources for arts-infused lesson materials across the K–8 curriculum is provided in Appendix A, Resource Bibliography, at the end of this book.)

First, we will revisit some of our contributing teachers' ideas concerning *how* and *why* they selected certain materials for their arts-infused, standards-based lessons across the curriculum.

Mr. Gonzalez's Lesson: Beyond Teaching Comfort Zones

As you may remember, Mr. Gonzalez's middle school lesson "Let's Find Out: George Washington and the American Revolutionary War" was purposely planned around what his students needed to know and remember. That is, standards-based facts about the history topic at hand. (See the "Lesson Tracker REPLAY" for a reminder about this lesson's content and focus.)

● l e s s o n t r a c k e r r e p l a y

Mr. Gonzalez's "Let's Find Out": George Washington and the American Revolutionary War"

Big Ideas

● Who was George Washington and what was the American Revolutionary war?

● What do students already know and what do they want to know about the topic?

● Students formulate questions, research, and participate in group arts activities based on answering their own questions about the topic.

Content Standards Addressed

● **Grade 8: U.S. History and Geography**—Understand major events preceding the founding of the nation; Understand the role of leaders such as George Washington.

● **Grade 8: English Language Arts**—Students read and respond to historically or culturally significant works of literature that reflect and enhance their studies of history and social science; deliver oral responses to literature.

● **Grade 8: Theatre**—Use theatrical skills to present content or concepts in other subject areas; write and create short dramatizations; perform character-based improvisations, pantomimes, or monologues.

● **Grade 8: Music**—Understand the historical contributions and cultural dimensions of music; identify and explain the influences of various cultures on music in early U.S. history; perform music from diverse genres, cultures, and time periods.

Within Mr. Gonzalez's "Big Ideas" and "Content Standards Addressed" sections in this "Lesson Tracker REPLAY," you find evidence that Mr. Gonzalez went well beyond his content area "comfort zone," of specialized teaching expertise (middle school history/social science). Through his own cycle of purposeful planning, Mr. Gonzalez sought to broaden the scope of his history lesson by first reading and understanding important interconnections imbedded within other content areas' standards-based learning contexts.

l e s s o n   t r a c k e r

Mr. Gonzalez's "Let's Find Out: George Washington and the American Revolutionary War"

Interdisciplinary, Standards-Based Contexts for Arts-Infused Learning

- *Literature/Language Arts:* Reading of informational text and biography about the topic; reader's theatre created from informational text
- *Oral Language Development:* Discussion, group work, oral presentations
- *Arts Activities:* Active learning involving direct participation in the following:
  - Music: Listening, group singing, patterned dance, historical song-text discussion and analysis
  - Visual Art: Observation and analysis of historical period paintings
  - Theatre: Acting/reenactments of historical characters and scenes, dramatic movement tableaux, group reader's theatre

Teacher Debriefing: Mr. Gonzalez's Connections Across Content Areas

Mr. Gonzalez explains why and how he broadened his grade 8 history lesson planning by considering grade-level standards in English Language Arts. *(Note his willingness to think about and locate materials for arts-infused activities outside his own teaching "comfort zone.")* He described the following:

> I read through the on-line State English Language Arts Standards for Grade 8 and found that students could "read, reflect, respond, create and do oral presentations to literature" linked to what we were studying in my History class (George Washington and the Revolutionary War). I began to get some ideas.
>
> How about Theatre? (Then my mental "search engine" instincts kicked in.) My kids need to "do" things and learn in an active and highly involved way. Could I design ways for my students to group research informational texts and biographical sources? Could they prepare their own re-telling of historical facts and then perform them dramatically for the whole group? I could see how this might work.
>
> My students needed motivation. I needed motivation. This period of history was a long time ago, and not very familiar (or interesting to them, to be quite honest). I knew my kids would love opportunities to work with peers. They need to be active

and involved to remember more historical facts and events. Middle School is all about activity and peer interaction.

I am not confident about teaching with the arts and do not have any solid arts experiences in my background. But I searched the State Music Content Standards anyway. I've always considered myself a non-singer. When I read the section about "understanding the historical contributions and cultural dimensions of music; identify and explain the influences of various cultures on music in early United States history; perform music from diverse genres, cultures, and time periods," the song "Yankee Doodle" came to me. It had been over 20 years since I sang that song, but I remembered it.

Then (with the help of our school's music teacher) I found a CD in a music text series to use to help me lead the song. The stronger singers in my class helped me along. They amazed me. As we sang, I got more ideas to incorporate a historically based reader's theatre about the song text of

4.1	More about Reader's Theatre

For further ideas about creating your own, customized reader's theatre materials, see Figure 4.1, "Tips for Creating Reader's Theatre Materials and Activity." *Note:* Mr. Gonzalez used a reader's theatre about the song "Yankee Doodle." See Chapter 1, Figure 1.3, "'Yankee Doodle' Reader's Theatre," by Nan L. McDonald.

"Yankee Doodle." I found one I remembered from a university methods course. [For more about reader's theatre, see the sidebar "More About Reader's Theatre" and Figure 4.1, "Tips for Creating Reader's Theatre Materials and Activity".]

So, I guess my "comfort zone" with the arts was expanded by reading and seeing some connections between content areas. I knew I could plan something that I could try as an experiment. And it worked.

In other words, Mr. Gonzalez expanded his teaching comfort zone well beyond his familiar instructional content territory. His understanding about what his students needed to know and to "do" to master and remember content about the topic at hand propelled him to find and incorporate important learning connections across other content area (Language Arts, Music, Theatre, Visual Art) standards. *His search for arts-infused materials became a natural outgrowth of the interdisciplinary connections he discovered and established related to what his students needed to know, do, and understand.*

Materials Planning Cycle

Mr. Gonzalez's candor about his comfort level (or lack thereof) with the arts was an important factor in his materials planning. This is a common experience for many classroom teachers. So is the perception that planning for and finding materials for arts infusion just takes too much time, special expertise, creativity and/or talent (McDonald & Fisher, 2002, 2006). If you, too, are caught in a similar way of thinking, what follows may be of help to you.

FIGURE 4.1   Tips for Creating Reader's Theatre Materials and Activity

Reader's theatre materials can be easily constructed from many sources: historical facts in student texts, informational text (i.e. biography), and children's literature and poetry (particularly those books with rhyming text and reoccurring text "refrains"). *(For more about reader's theatre materials, teaching ideas, and activities, see the resource bibliography in the Appendix of this book.)*

In preparing appropriate materials for reader's theatre activities for students, simply assign (number the sections on the printed text of the reader's theatre) *solo* reader parts in combination and alteration with *small groups of readers* and *whole-group refrains* (or repeating text sections). *This variety of voice groupings creates interesting and engaging (musical/theatrical) reading and oral language opportunities for students to use their voices in expressive, creative, artistic, and imaginative ways!*

Encourage your students to do the following:

- **Experiment with varying speaking dynamics** (range of loud and soft) as they read
- **Use different speeds in speaking** (contrasts in tempo and rhythms of speech)
- **Vary sound color** (i.e., voice timbre, e.g., deep voice, whisper, animated voice, etc.) **appropriately to match the meaning and feeling of the spoken words** within both individual and group parts
- **Use expressive voice inflection, accented words, and clear enunciation** to improve and develop their oral language skills as they make the "words come alive."

● BEYOND THE CLASSROOM ....

Peer Dialogue or Small-Group Reflection: Comfort Zones in Using the Arts

Use your responses to the "Focus Activity" survey at the beginning of this chapter to get a conversation going. Talk with others about their background and comfort zones in finding and using arts materials and activities in their own classroom. Start a conversation with a methods class or school-site peer, or even your school's arts specialist or district arts resource teacher. Talk about your background, thoughts, and experiences and listen to others as they describe their own.

First, let's carefully re-consider all that Mr. Gonzalez achieved in his planning cycle. In spite of his honestly admitted limitations, he was driven by an even stronger desire to make his arts-infused teaching within active learning episodes more *meaningful and memorable* for his students (Cornett, 2006; Frey & Fisher, 2007; Hancock, 2007; McDonald, 2007; McDonald & Fisher, 2000, 2002, 2004, 2006; Rosenblatt, 1995). He searched until he found and understood important *interdisciplinary connections* (Jacobs, 1989, 1997) and contexts between standards-based learning in History/Social Science, English Language Arts, and in Theatre, Music, and Visual Arts.

Mr. Gonzalez's: "Let's Find Out: George Washington and the American Revolutionary War"

Mr. Gonzalez's Materials Planning Cycle

- Revisit overall, standards-based purposeful plan.
- Consider student needs for learning.
- Search and consider other content standards (including the Arts) at the same grade level.
- Imagine and consider (pre-plan) possible arts-infused lesson activity appropriate to purposeful planning goals.
- Select and locate appropriate materials he already has and knows (and/or can easily find).
- Search and locate other resources checking for appropriateness and usefulness matched to his own purposeful planning criteria.

Mr. Gonzalez took the following sequence of purposeful planning steps as he searched for materials needed to teach his arts-infused lesson:

1. Mentally revisited his plan, "what students need to know," and re-read his grade-level History/Social Science content standards for his topic

2. Found out *what students already knew* (through class discussions) and *what they wanted to know* (students formulated their own questions about the topic) and used that information to shape and categorize his eventual search for materials

3. Considered and planned around his middle school student's needs to use oral language, develop background and vocabulary, and learn and remember through interesting small-group research activity

4. Considered his student's needs as a catalyst to search for connections to other grade-level-appropriate, standards-based learning (e.g., English Language Arts)

5. Found connections to potential active arts activities imbedded in these content area standards

6. Researched and considered grade-level standards in Arts content areas: Theatre, Music, and Visual Art (outside his immediate "comfort zone")

7. Imagined and pre-planned potential arts-infused lesson activities appropriate to his purposeful planning goals (e.g., reader's theatre, singing, analysis of visual art, etc., related to his topic and student's needs)

8. Used "what he already knew" and searched for and found materials easily available and accessible at his school site (e.g., library, computer search, peer discussion with music teacher, etc.) to help formulate active arts activities linked to his history content lesson-planning goals

Importantly, because Mr. Gonzalez was able to reference and revisit his own planning goals and processes (just as you have done throughout this book), *his search for useful connections and materials became clearer, easier to accomplish, and less time-consuming.* He was able to see that *content standards often include implicit and explicit connections to learning contexts related to content in other subject matters.*

Planning Interdisciplinary Activities to Connect Students to Other Learning

A bigger picture comes into view. Mr. Gonzalez instinctively knew the importance of creating materials and designing interdisciplinary activities to *connect students to other learning they experience throughout their school day and beyond* (Jacobs, 1989).

Through his purposefully planned and selected materials and activities, Mr. Gonzalez helped his grade 8 students to establish *natural* and *valid* connections between their arts activity (Music, Visual Art, Theatre), other content (English Language Arts), and the American History/Social Science topic at hand. Through this active arts-infusion, Mr. Gonzalez's students were able to learn in more meaningful and memorable ways.

In addition to engaging students within specific learning parameters defined by the various Arts content standards, you might consider creating interdisciplinary opportunities for students to experience deeper understandings of the arts through "the intersections and interactions of the disciplines" (Barrett, 2001, p. 27). Seen in this context, the arts become integrated with each other and with other subject areas "as an active way to enhance overall instruction, not to compete or replace discipline specific teaching and learning" (McDonald & Fisher, 2002, p. 13).

Furthermore, Mr. Gonzalez's purposeful choice of materials and eventual arts-infused lesson activities connected his students to other learning and life experiences in the following ways:

- Through asking students what they already knew about the topic (Ogle, 1986)
- Through utilizing *visual literacy techniques* (paintings of the period, music and song-text media, being an audience for other's historical reenactments, etc.) in analysis discussions and group presentations (Frey & Fisher, 2007; Lapp, Flood, & Fisher, 1999; McDonald & Fisher, 2002, 2006)

- Through providing *multiple learning modalities* within active participation in purposeful, interdisciplinary arts activities (Cornett, 2006; Hancock, 2007; McDonald, 2008; McDonald & Fisher, 2002, 2004, 2006; Snyder, 2001)

Summary: Mr. Gonzalez's Purposeful Materials Planning

While reading this chapter, you have probably begun to think about your own integrated arts lessons, as well as how you will select appropriate resources. As you read, Mr. Gonzalez thought a lot about ways to fully engage his students and connect them to (and remember) historical facts about the topic at hand. He also thought about ways to connect students to their peers and draw upon their previous experiences across the school curriculum and beyond.

Mr. Gonzalez's willingness to try new activities in his history class propelled him to search for interesting, engaging, and appropriate materials for his arts-infused history lesson. He candidly reflected upon his planning processes in an open and constructive manner—one that will undoubtedly contribute to increased confidence in finding and using materials for future arts-infused learning activities in his classroom.

Finally, Mr. Gonzalez remained true to his own purposeful planning as he sought, found, and used materials related to what his students needed to know and remember. As a result of his purposeful planning, he met his original goal: *He successfully implemented creative ways for his students to learn, understand, and remember more historically based facts through their active participation in meaningful arts activities linked to the topic at hand.*

As you may remember from Chapter 1, Mr. Gonzalez's student achievement increased in both class assessments and on standardized tests related to George Washington and the Revolutionary War. His students enjoyed their lesson activities (reported through discussion and written lesson reflection), and they asked for more of the same kinds of activity. Mr. Gonzalez learned with and through his students' shared experiences.

Selecting Appropriate Resources: Interviews With Other Contributing Teachers

As you know, the cycles of purposeful planning processes you have completed are directly matched to the processes used by our contributing teachers. Let's turn our attention back to what other contributing teachers have to say about their search and selection of appropriate resources.

Four of our contributing teachers—Mr. Pham, Mrs. Gray, Ms. Elemont, and Ms. Tanonis—were each asked the same six questions during one-on-one interviews. The questions were as follows:

- What arts are within your personal "comfort zone" and why? How do you choose to use them in your classroom?
- Once you've determined which art(s) to use, where do you go or what do you do to begin to look for materials?
- Examples of favorite materials?
- When you locate a resource of some kind, *how* you determine if it's right for your students' needs?
- Does it matter to you that integrated arts materials come with an explanation of "how to use them"? Why or why not?
- If you could wish for the ideal resource (people, place, or thing) for your integrated arts-infused lessons, what would it include?

What follows are highlights from their responses to the questions above.

Interview with Mr. Pham (Grades 4 and 5)

Khanh Pham teaches both grade 4 and grade 5. One of Mr. Pham's lesson examples can be found in Chapter 2. This interdisciplinary lesson is entitled "Integrating Social Studies (History/Geography), Math, and the Arts: "'Exploration/Colonization'" and includes the following standards-based content areas: History/Social Science, Math, and Arts (Visual Art).

When asked about his *personal comfort zone* in using the arts, Mr. Pham said he "preferred visual art projects to get the kids hands-on with what they are learning in a very physical, direct, and tactile way." He also likes to "use movement and music to create high interest" in his classroom to "achieve total physical involvement."

When asked about *materials,* Mr. Pham said he keeps his "supplemental" (arts-infusion) materials in a file he's created and kept active since his first year of teaching. He also consults Scholastic catalogs and any other catalog (online or hard copy) he can find. He does web searches at the Scholastic website, where he searches for "supplemental books related to whatever topic I am teaching."

When asked how he looks for supplemental books and lesson plans online, Mr. Pham adds, "I just Google search by typing in the name of the topic, like 'explora-

FIGURE 4.2 Eight Considerations for Selecting Quality Websites

As you search for materials, use the following "yes/no" checklist to evaluate the quality of each web (online) resource you review.

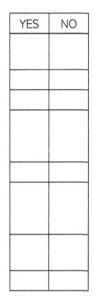

	YES	NO
1. Is the Web resource linked to your purposeful planning goals, particularly concerning "what students need to know"?		
2. Was this Web resource written by an educator and/or expert(s) in the field?		
3. Is this Web resource current and relevant to the topic at hand?		
4. Does the Web resource offer interesting, standards-based content in language matched to student's literacy skill levels and art-activity experience level? If not, are you able to translate to match your students' needs?		
5. Is the Web resource content interesting and easy for both you and your students to use?		
6. Does the Web resource offer graphics, artwork, sound bites, and other opportunities to develop visual literacy and creative activities to enhance and enrich teaching and learning across content areas?		
7. Can you easily imagine arts-infused lessons and assessments linked to (and using) this Web resource?		
8. Does the Web resource establish other links of similar quality?		

tion, colonization lessons,' and then I look for any and all lessons which feature arts lesson activities and materials."

Some of Mr. Pham's *criteria for choosing appropriate materials* focuses around whether or not those materials are

matched to my inner-city students' English second language needs and their levels in reading, writing, and speaking. I like websites that are easy to read and have pictures and captions, not tons of information and too rich text. Then, I ask myself whether the material covers the specific needs of my kids and if *I* can then actually tailor the materials I see to those needs.

For more information about selecting appropriate websites, see Figure 4.2, "Eight Considerations for Selecting Quality Websites." (For more catalogs and websites, see the Resource Bibliography in the Appendix of this book.)

Mr. Pham expressed that the *ideal resource* would be "people." To this he added,

That means *other teachers.* A group of people like those on our school site Integrated Arts Curriculum Team who are given time to regularly meet to exchange ideas and work on strategies for developing our own ideas. We need professional dialogues and opportunities to share out. I learn best from other teachers.

I also get a lot of ideas from the experiences we've had where university students (future classroom teachers and arts specialists) come and model pilot lessons in my classroom and share their written lesson plans and materials lists. I give the university students specific feedback and comments as part of their overall grade for their field experiences in my classroom. My kids and I really learned a lot from these arts experiences.

Interview With Mrs. Gray (Grade 3)

Kate Gray teaches grade 3. One of Mrs. Gray's lesson examples, entitled "Integrating Social Studies (Geography) and the Arts: "Desert Habitat Art," can be found in Chapter 2, and the standards-based content areas included are History/Social Science (Geography) and Arts (Visual Art).

Mrs. Gray's comfort zone with the arts naturally includes music and movement (dance), as those avenues are "matched to my students' literacy needs and they get a great deal of enjoyment out of all. I get the most 'bang for my buck' when I teach with music and movement, as those arts cover a lot of teaching territory."

> **4.2 Text series and Teaching Resources in the Arts for Your Materials Planning:**
>
> For more texts and resources for teaching with the Arts across the curriculum, see Appendix A, Resource Bibliography.

Concerning specific materials, Mrs. Gray is very comfortable in using the district- and school-site-adopted K-8 text series and CDs in music. She located the most current edition in her school library and also attended several local university and district workshops designed to help classroom teachers use those materials. "Once I learned to use the series' Master Index, I could find music materials, listening ideas, poetry, and movement linked to any of my grade-level curriculum themes. This is incredibly helpful."

When asked about her *criteria for selecting appropriate materials*, Mrs. Gray looks for

specific material needed. Then, I ask myself, "How long will this take?" I *have* to know what I'm getting into in terms of time even before I review the material or try a lesson idea. So a resource that describes lesson time perimeters is *very* helpful to me.

Mrs. Gray's idea of an *ideal resource* would be one that

features children's literature connections to the arts. I want to see finished visual arts projects done by both the teacher and some by real students to show to my kids as a motivator. I want them to think, "a kid did this, so I can too." There would be photographs of students in action at the different stages of the projects. The standards across the curriculum would be listed and there would be suggestions of how to assess that learning.

Finally, Mrs. Gray mirrors Mr. Pham's reflection that people are a huge resource toward her classroom arts activity. She shares Mr. Pham's enthusiasm for the lab lessons by visiting (undergraduate) students from a local university.

> Through watching the future arts specialists, in particular, I could really understand the arts standards in action. Those future teachers taught my kids and I a *lot* of terminology, procedures, and applications and we got to use new vocabulary in an active way.

Interview With Ms. Elemont (Grade 6 Math)

Christi Elemont is a new educator and currently teaches sixth-grade math. You read about one of her lessons, entitled "Integrating Math and the Arts: Measuring and Classifying Angles through Dance," in Chapter 2. The content areas in this lesson include Math (Measurement and Geometry) and the art of Dance.

When asked about her *comfort zone and preference* in which arts to use in her classroom, Ms. Elemont explains,

> It depends on the lesson. My goal is to make learning as *active* as possible. Active . . . [she's thinking] . . . and I want my kids to be able to *create* something.
>
> Geometry goes perfectly with dance with the emphasis on angles and shapes, lines, direction. Dance activity in my geometry units allow my kids to make up their own interpretations of what we are studying. That's how they remember geometry—by re-creating geometry *through their bodies.*
>
> I'm most comfortable with song activities and rhythmic chant, as I can match those easily with math terms and procedures. You know, I watch my kids carefully during tests of all kinds. They often move their lips as they answer questions. I know they are recalling math terms in the rhythmic sequences we chanted and danced. Those words have become part of them, and they are in their bodies.
>
> At the end of the year, my kids asked "Can we sing *all* the (math) songs from the entire year?" Now, how many times do sixth graders beg to review information from more traditional lessons? Never.

Ms. Elemont explains her *criteria for choosing appropriate materials* for her planning goals by emphasizing the following:

> You know, I need to see if the students will be *engaged* in the materials and lesson activities. Will they be moving around? Will they be able to talk to each other? Will they

really be involved, paying attention, and interested/motivating in what they need to know?

I look for good teaching strategies adaptable to my needs. I need to focus on vocabulary and graphic organizers. So, basically, I ask myself, "What can I do to this resource to make it fit my needs?

Interview With Ms. Tanonis (Grades K and 1)

Rose Tanonis has taught both kindergarten and grade 1.

You read about one of her lessons, entitled "Integrating Science and the Arts: Lifecycle of Butterflies," in Chapter 2 pages 27–55. The following content areas were included: Science, English Language Arts (Reading, Author Study, Oral Language), and Arts (Visual Art).

Ms. Tanonis has an interesting and unusual educational background. She is an inner-city K/1 classroom teacher who has background in the visual arts (i.e., an undergraduate major in visual art–painting, printmaking, and photography). Ms. Tanonis loves being able to use those skills within her own classroom curriculum and within rotating arts integration lessons with children from several grade 1 classes at her school site. (Note: Many of you may wish this kind of arts integration rotation could be started at your school site or future school site. This and other ideas for peer collaboration appear later in this book, in Chapter 8, "Arts Within My Classroom and Beyond.")

Ms. Tanonis had a lot to say about *attitude* needed in teaching another, less comfortable art for her—music.

Positive energy goes a long way with my kids. It is infectious. I have a smile on my face and make our song be "ours." I pretend I am an opera teacher and just belt out the song with confidence. I am fearless. My class loves this. I type up the lyrics which I purposely choose to match their literacy level. I sell the excitement and importance of singing through my own excitement.

When asked where she finds *materials,* Ms. Tanonis said, "They can be anywhere. I have learned to teach to the media I find." One of her favorite websites for teaching visual art rotations is www.arhstportfolio.net. She advises that,

There are usually great art materials in every district, but classroom teachers need to search for these at district resource centers or the school-site libraries. Start by asking where the art books are.

Text series in Art (like the ones in Music) give me a lot of age-appropriate ideas and lesson structures/materials to use. Many of them also have transparencies of works of visual art tied to curriculum themes by grade level. They have great project ideas too. There are Teacher Edition books and materials for each grade, and they are matched to the standards and themes across the curriculum. I love using these sources, because when I find something new, I can just grab what I need.

Another thing I do is online is search by typing in the actual name of an artist like "Van Gogh," and I'll be instantly taken to many websites with great lesson ideas and materials for using visual art across the curriculum."

Finally, Ms. Tanonis offered the following advice,

The greatest thing to do is to take kids to the museum. Know about the art there before you go. Ask docents for help. And another thing, as kids, my brother and I *did* art every day. This shaped me and made me love art.

Summary of Contributing Teachers' Considerations and Criteria for Materials Planning

Mr. Pham, Mrs. Gray, Ms. Elemont, and Ms. Tanonis each candidly described both their personal *comfort levels with the arts* as well as their *criteria* for choosing their arts activity materials. And, as you read, they did so in a highly diversified and personalized manner. Although each set of answers was unique to that individual, their composite ideas (complete interview data) about the search for materials can be correlated within the descriptive categories presented in Figure 4.3.

Within the four contributing teacher interviews, you also noticed the teachers' references to the same *purposeful planning questions* we've covered in this book:

- Big Ideas: What do my students need to know? (Wiggins & McTighe, 2006)
- What are the content standards involved?
- What do my students already know?
- How can arts activities be used to help bridge gaps in student understanding?
- *Why, how,* and *what* can students learn through arts-infusion activities across the curriculum?

You will revisit these same questions as you now begin your personalized search for your arts-infused lesson materials.

FIGURE 4.3 Teacher Considerations/Criteria for Materials Planning

The following list is a condensation of data about what classroom teachers consider when they search for materials for arts-infused lessons across the curriculum. The list is compiled from one-on-one interviews with this book's contributing teachers and from written data from over 50 K–8 classroom teachers' contributing to *Teaching Literacy through the Arts* by Nan L. McDonald and Douglas Fisher (2006, Guilford).

Considerations: Personal Background of Teacher

- Educational background and teaching experience
- Personal arts comfort zone and preferred types of arts activities leadership

Considerations: Background of Students' Instructional Needs

- Grade level/subject area
- Grade level content area standards
- Students' achievement level and needs
- Students' literacy skills (reading, writing, oral language)
- Students' background and previous experience in arts activities (music, dance, theatre, visual art)
- Students' special needs (e.g., varied learning modalities, total physical response, ELL, Special Learners/Inclusion, Gifted and Talented)

Considerations: Possible "Resources" for Arts-Infused Lessons Across the K-8 Curriculum

- *People, places, and things*—All are resources for arts-infused lesson materials.
- *Materials* can be found in the following contexts and more:
  - Arts education K-8 texts and text series
  - Arts and university-integrated arts methods books
  - Higher education course-work materials and model lessons
  - Online units and lesson plans
  - In catalogs
  - On-site in classrooms
  - On-site with peers
  - Parents and community
  - School and public libraries
  - District resource centers and libraries
  - District arts coordinators or resource teachers
  - Teacher supply retail outlets
  - Community arts-education providers
  - Local museum educators

- Local university arts education programs, performances, and teaching internships (pilot lessons)

Criteria: Questions for Locating Appropriate Resources

- How are found or existing arts-infused materials linked to the purposefully planned, grade-level/standards-based topic or instructional theme at hand?
- Do found or existing materials match or exceed student literacy levels?
- Do materials have potential for use in hands-on, active, engaged, memorable, arts-infused classroom activities linked to student learning needs?
- Will these materials and resulting activity be of meaningful interest to students?
- Are materials easy to obtain, usable, and "doable" within future activities?
- Can materials be easily used considering the teacher's arts comfort zone, experience, skill, and confidence level?
- Do materials contain easy-to-read, clear instructions, and lesson ideas/procedures not in thick rich-text format?
- Do materials include photographs of students engaged in the actual learning stages of the arts activity?
- Do materials include an actual student-completed sample of the arts-based project or activity?
- Can materials be used within teacher time restraints and demands?
- Can materials be adapted and personalized for varying student and class needs?

The Role of Teacher Attitude

- Does the teacher have a willingness to experiment in searching for, creating, and using a variety of arts materials and activities in his or her classroom?

Conclusion

This chapter continued to layer the cycles of arts-infused lesson planning through emphasis on the next stage—your search for resources that are *appropriate to your needs and the needs of your students* and therefore *matched to your own purposeful plan.*

Your selection of resources can be simultaneously accompanied by a "thought cycle" (pre-planning) about the actual arts activities you might use in your arts-infused lesson(s). According to classroom teacher data, this is a common experience. In fact, many teachers report that they think of potential activities first, then search for appropriate materials, and finally loop back to planning the activities using those carefully chosen materials (McDonald & Fisher, 2006). It's now time for you to explore the same self-study processes in selecting appropriate resources.

Self-Study Exercises

You may wish to jot down any and all arts activity ideas that come to mind as you complete the materials planning exercises and criteria checklist at the end of this chapter.

● BEYOND THE CLASSROOM ....

Prepare for Your Own "Creativity Surge"

Creative ideas often come to us when we are engaged in other activities. Be prepared to let your ideas freely flow out of the lesson-materials planning discussions, self-study, and criteria checklist activities at the end of this chapter. Keep some sticky notes handy, so when the following arts materials/activities and other ideas come to mind, you will be prepared to record your ideas:

- Arts activities matched to your students' needs
- Resources you already have at home or school
- District and school-site resources
- Websites, catalogs
- Teaching magazines and catalogs
- Persons you might ask for particular materials or expertise
- A teacher you remember who has _____ materials and great ideas for _____ activities
- Local community and university arts-education resources, etc.

....

Figure 4.5, "Materials Criteria Checklist," provided at the end of this chapter, can be copied and *used over and over again* as you review *each* potential resource or materials for your arts-infused lesson(s). This particular list was created to include what many classroom teachers have identified as important criteria in their search for appropriate, purposefully planned materials. *However, if you think of a more useful design for your needs (with your purposeful planning stages in mind), create and design your own customized checklist and share it with peers.* This activity could be used as an interesting assignment or small-group exercise in your university methods class.

The construction of your resource search and selection process began when you read and discussed your arts-infused ideas in Chapter 1. You undoubtedly continued to think about appropriate materials during your written work on self-study worksheets at the end of both Chapter 2 and Chapter 3. (Suggestion: If you haven't completed these worksheets, do so now.) The foundations you have laid in your own purposeful planning for your arts-infused lesson(s) will now propel you, much like Mr. Gonzalez and our other teachers, to construct an enjoyable, informed search and successful selection of appropriate resources.

You now have the opportunity to participate in a suggested peer discussion, answer a short *self-study* survey, and use a *materials criteria checklist* for your own search and selection of appropriate resources for your arts-infused lesson(s). (Reminder: the Appendix: Resource Bibliography, contains many resources appropriate for your needs, including texts, articles, websites, teacher books, children's literature, other media, people, places, and things.)

Suggestions for Peer Discussions

- *Find a peer or two:* Select one or more peers in your methods class or school site. Agree to have a professional discussion in which each person gets "equal time." *These dialogues could also take the form of a phone or email conversation.*

- *Pick a time frame:* Decide how much time you have for this discussion (live, phone, or online).

- *Structure the content of your discussion:* Use the "agree/disagree" statements you answered in the Focus Activity at the very beginning of this chapter. (If you did not respond to the statements *before* you read this chapter, do so now in the "after" column, and a discussion can still work!)

- *Stay on topic:* One statement at a time, share your responses (either "before" *and* "after" reading the chapter, or just "after"). It might be best to stay on one statement at a time until *each* person has responded to that *one* idea. Go to the next response, with everyone offering their ideas, and so on.

- *Use constructivist listening techniques in reflective practice dialogues/discussions* (McDonald, 2000; Meier, 1996; Mezirow, 1990, 1997; Schon, 1991): Be sure to allow all participants to talk (or write) without interruptions, conversations, or suggestions, etc. (those opportunities will come later). Allow yourself and peers a chance to be fully "heard." In live conversations, you might want to keep track of the time so no one person will use more time than others. As we all know, this can be problematic in equitable discussions.

- *Feedback:* Once everyone is "heard," allow time to freely respond to each other in true dialogue: back-and-forth questions and answers, brainstorming, suggestions, and ideas. Remember to focus on your dual role as both a "receiver" and "giver" of suggestions. Listen and talk.

- *Memory of the Peer Discussion* (McDonald & Fisher 2000, 2002, 2006): Take notes on what others suggest to you, as rich ideas can flow out of constructive peer dialogue and small-group discussions.

Suggestions for Completing Figure 4.4, "Self-Study: Resource Planning and Selection"

To prepare for your materials search, you will need to *revisit the purposeful planning* you have already accomplished about your arts-infused lesson(s).

- Take time now to carefully re-read and/or revisit your written ideas on the self-study worksheets from previous chapters:
- Chapter 1, Table 1.2, "Activities Students Can Do in the Four Arts" Chapter 2, Figure 2.1, "Self-Study: 'What Students Need to Know'"
- Chapter 3, Figure 3.3, "Self-Study: 'What Students Already Know'"
- Consult this past planning to help answer the questions about the selection of quality resources.
- Fill in the Figure 4.4 worksheet, "Self Study: Resource Planning and Selection," and be sure to keep or store your work.
- Be sure you fill in the section of this self-study involving arts-infused activity ideas in which to use the materials you will find. These responses will become very important toward the next chapter's focus on instruction.

FIGURE 4.4   Self-Study: Resource Planning and Selection

Instructions for using this self-study:

- Make copies of this blank form as needed.
- Fill in the following worksheet *before* you begin using Figure 4.5, "Materials Criteria Checklist," in your search for resources.
- You will need to search (online or hard copy) your grade level/content area instructional standards including standards in the Arts. Keep this information handy.
- Keep or store your work on this self-study worksheet.

Name: _____   Date: _____

Methods Class/Grade/Subject: _____

School Site: _____

Topic or Your Arts-Infused Lesson(s) Theme: _____

Content Area(s): _____

Art or arts you plan to use: _____   _____   _____

_____   _____

I. Considerations: Your Background

Which arts are within your personal comfort zone? Why?

What kinds of arts activities do you like to lead in your classroom? Why?

II. *Your Arts-Infused Lesson* Materials Planning Considerations: Background of Student's Instructional Needs

IMPORTANT NOTE: The following information concerns the arts-infused lesson(s) you have been planning throughout this book.

Grade Level/Subject Area: _____

Grade-level content area standards to be involved (#s): _____

_____

_____

Student's achievement level in this content: _____

_____

. . . .

95

Student's overall literacy skill levels (reading, writing, speaking): _____

_____

Grade-Level Arts Standards (#s) I could possibly link to and use within my arts-infused lesson:
(NOTE: You will need to refer to your State Arts Content Standards linked to the grade level of your arts-infused lesson(s).

Music: _____
Why? _____
Dance: _____
Why? _____
Theatre: _____
Why? _____
Visual Arts: _____
Why? _____

The student's background and previous experience in arts activities (music, dance, theatre, visual art):

Music: _____

Dance: _____

Theatre: _____

Visual Arts: _____

What are some actual arts activities you have in mind for this/these lesson(s)? (briefly list here)

1. _____
2. _____
3. _____
4. _____
5. _____

Briefly describe *how* you might address various students' learning needs (i.e., varied learning modalities, total physical response, ELL, Special Learners/Inclusion, Gifted and Talented) within the above potential arts-infused lesson activities:

_____

_____

_____

(continued)

Suggestions for Completing Figure 4.4, "Self-Study: Resource Planning and Selection"

FIGURE 4.4   (continued)

III. Possible "Resources" for Your Arts-Infused Lessons Across the K-8 Curriculum

Note: People, places, and things—all are resources for arts-infused lesson materials. Materials can be found within the following contexts and more.

INSTRUCTIONS: Place a CHECK next to the following items below that *you intend to consider* for your materials search for your own arts-infused lesson(s). Be sure to find and fill in as much information you can about items of interest to you.

People

❐ Methods class or teaching peers (who?): _____

❐ School librarian (who?): _____

❐ District arts coordinators or resource teachers (who?): _____

_____

❐ Community artists you know or know of (who?): _____

_____

❐ Community arts-education providers (list possible providers here): _____

_____

❐ Local museum educators (list names of museums here): _____

_____

❐ Local community college, college, and/or university arts education programs (list name of university and any possible contacts here):

_____

_____

Places

❐ Master teachers' classrooms

❐ My classroom

❐ Peers' classrooms (list): _____

❐ University or school-site Library

❐ District resource centers and libraries (list names and locations):

_____

_____

❐ School or district arts resources list (names/location of lists):

_____

_____

❐ Local teacher supply retail outlets (list):

_____

❒ Local museums/historical societies (list):

_____

_____

❒ Your community arts venues and performance series (list):

_____

_____

❒ Local high school, community college, college, and/or university arts departments and events (list):

_____

_____

Things

❒ My professional file, ideas, and collection of arts materials in my own classroom

❒ My peers' files, ideas, and materials

❒ School-site arts supplies and resources (list location of appropriate supplies):

_____

❒ District-state-adopted arts education K–8 texts and text series/media (list names of text series _and_ location): _____

_____

❒ Arts/integrated arts methods books (list):

_____

_____

❒ Higher education coursework materials and model lessons (list):

_____

_____

❒ Teaching journals or magazines (list):

_____

_____

❒ Websites (list website addresses and brief notes on what they contain):

_____

_____

❒ Online units and lesson plans (list website addresses and brief notes on that they contain):

_____

_____

❒ Catalogs (List names of hard copy and/or on-line catalogs)

_____

_____

Suggestions for Completing Figure 4.4, "Self-Study: Resource Planning and Selection"

Suggestions for Using Figure 4.5, "Materials Criteria Checklist"

After you have completed your responses in Figure 4.4, "Self Study: Resource Planning and Selection," here are suggestions for how to use the Figure 4.5 "Materials Criteria Checklist" for each potential resource you may choose to use in your arts-infused lesson(s):

- Before you begin, make 5 to 10 copies of the blank "Materials Criteria Checklist" form. Do not write your answers on this book's pages, as you may want to duplicate and use this form in the future. You need one copy for each resource you review.
- Begin searching for existing or found materials for your lesson(s). Search for at least five different kinds of resources for your lesson(s)
- Once you think of or locate each resource, fill in *one* checklist about that *one* resource, and so on.
- Do the same for at least five different resources/materials you find for your arts-infused content lesson(s).
- Keep your checklists with your other purposeful planning paperwork (hard copy or stored in your computer files).
- Finally, if you are so inclined, create your own version of a materials criteria checklist for personal use. Compare and share customized checklists with others.

FIGURE 4.5   Materials Criteria Checklist

How to use this checklist:

- Make multiple copies of this blank checklist (at least 5).
- Use one checklist for each resource you find and are considering for your arts-infused lesson(s).
- Follow the order of the checklist's considerations.
- Next to each category, simply check "yes" or "no" to the left of that statement.
- Some categories provide room for a short written response. Fill in as much as you can.
- Aim to review at least 5 potential resources per arts-infused lesson idea.
- Keep your paperwork or store on your computer. You will need to use these lists in Chapter 5, "Instruction."

Name: _____   Date: _____

University Methods Class/Grade/Subject: _____

School Site: _____

Your Arts-Infused Topic or Lesson Theme: _____

Content Area(s) Involved (non-Arts): _____

List your grade-level content standards (#s) addressed (non-arts):

_____

_____

List the *Arts* you plan to infuse into this lesson:

_____

_____

List the grade-level arts content standards (#s) addressed:

_____

_____

Name of this particular material or resource:

_____

_____

Location of this material:

_____

_____

Criteria: Questions for Locating Appropriate Materials

Yes	No
❏	❏

Does this found or existing arts resource link well to my purposefully planned, grade-level/standards-based topic or instructional theme at hand? If yes, how?

_____

_____

_____

Which arts are contained within this material?

_____

_____

_____

(continued)

Suggestions for Using Figure 4.5, "Materials Criteria Checklist"

FIGURE 4.5   (continued)

Yes	No	
❐	❐	Does this material match or exceed my student literacy levels?
❐	❐	Does this material have potential for use in hands-on, active, engaged, memorable, arts-infused classroom activities linked to student learning needs I articulated in my planning? If yes, how?
		_____
		_____
		_____
❐	❐	Will this material and potential activity be of meaningful interest to my students?
❐	❐	Is this material easy to obtain, usable, and "doable" in my classroom?
❐	❐	Can this material be easily used considering my comfort zone with the arts, experience, skill, and confidence level?
❐	❐	Does this material contain easy-to-read, clear instructions, and lesson ideas/procedures not in thick rich-text format?
❐	❐	Does this material also include photographs of students engaged in the actual learning stages of the arts activity?
❐	❐	Does this material include an actual student-completed sample of the arts-based project or activity?
❐	❐	Can this material be used within my time restraints and teaching demands?
❐	❐	Can this material be adapted and personalized for my varying student and class needs? If yes, how?
		_____
		_____
		_____

Attitude

Am I willing to experiment in using and/or adapting _this_ material within potential arts-infused activities in my classroom? If yes, why?

_____

_____

_____

If yes, how? Within what kinds of arts activity? (briefly list all potential ideas)

_____

_____

_____

_____

_____

References

Barrett, J. (2001). Interdisciplinary work and musical integrity. *Music Educators Journal, 87*(5), 27–31.

Cornett, C. (2006). *Creating meaning through literature and the arts: An integration resource for classroom teachers* (3rd ed.). Upper Saddle River, NJ: Prentice Hall.

Frey, N., & Fisher, D. (2007). *Reading for information in elementary school: Content literacy strategies to build comprehension.* Upper Saddle River, NJ: Merrill/Prentice Hall.

Hancock, M. (2007). *A celebration of literature and response: Children, books, and teachers in K-8 classrooms* (2nd ed.). Upper Saddle River, NJ: Prentice Hall.

Jacobs, H. H. (1989). *Interdisciplinary curriculum: Design and implementation.* Alexandria, VA: Association for Supervision and Curriculum Development.

Jacobs, H. H. (1997). *Mapping the big picture: Integrating curriculum and assessment K-12.* Alexandria, VA: Association for Supervision and curriculum Development.

Lapp, D., Flood, J., & Fisher, D. (1999). Intermediality: How the use of multiple media enhances learning. *The Reading Teacher, 52,* 776–780.

McDonald, N. (2000). Constructivist listening: Real-life classroom management and discipline concerns. *General Music Today, 13*(2), 3–7.

McDonald, N. (2008). Standards in the Arts and Arts within literacy instruction. In J. Flood, S. Brice-Heath, & D. Lapp (Eds.), *The Handbook of Research on Teaching Literacy Through the Communicative, Performing, and Visual Arts Volume II: Sponsored by the International Reading Association* (pp. 567–572). Mahwah, NJ: Lawrence Erlbaum.

McDonald, N., & Fisher, D. (1999). Living haiku: Scenes of sound in motion. In S. Totten, C. Johnson, L. R. Morrow, and T. Sills-Briegel (Eds.), *Practicing what we preach: Preparing middle level educators* (pp. 273–275). New York: Palmer.

McDonald, N., & Fisher, D. (2000). Tell them I sing: A dialogue on integrating curricula. *General Music Today, 14*(1), 13–18.

McDonald, N., & Fisher, D. (2002). *Developing arts-loving readers: Top ten questions teachers are asking about integrated arts education.* Lanham, MD: Rowman & Littlefield Education.

McDonald, N., & Fisher, D. (2004). Stormy weather: Leading Purposeful curriculum integration with and through the arts. *Teaching Artist Journal, 2*(4), 240–248.

McDonald, N., & Fisher, D. (2006). *Teaching literacy through the arts.* New York: Guilford.

Meier, D. (1996). Supposing that. *Phi Delta Kappan, 78*(4), 271–276.

Mezirow, J. (1997). Transformative learning: Theory to practice. *New Directions for Adult and Continuing Education, 74,* 5–12.

Mezirow, J. (1990). *Fostering critical reflection in adulthood: A guide to transformative and emancipatory learning.* San Francisco: Jossey-Bass.

Ogle, D. (1986). K-W-L: A teaching model that develops active reading of expository text. *The Reading Teacher, 39,* 564–570.

Rosenblatt, L. (1995). *Literature as exploration.* New York: Modern Language Association.

Schon, D. (1991). *The reflective turn: Case studies in and on educational practices.* New York: Teachers College Press.

Snyder, S. (2001). Connection, correlation, and integration. *Music Educators Journal, 87*(5), 32–39.

Wiggins, G., & McTighe, J. (2006). *Understanding by design Handbook* (2nd ed.). Alexandria, VA: Association for Supervision and Curriculum Development.

Instruction

Imagine a classroom where there are no right answers but a range of possible responses. Imagine a classroom where praise is replaced by coaching in the form of descriptive feedback offered by peers as often as teachers. Imagine a classroom where engagement is not manipulated through the use of points or coupons but happens because the arts hold natural appeal. These are not imaginary classrooms but classrooms that are driven by a passion for helping students realize their own full meaning-making capacities—possible only when the arts are central teaching and learning tools.

—Claudia E. Cornett (2006), "Center Stage: Arts-Based Read-Alouds"

Directions: Please fill out before and after reading this chapter.

Before Reading Chapter A = agree D = disagree	Statements	After Reading Chapter A = agree D = disagree
	I have had some positive experiences teaching arts activities.	
	Arts-activity infusion requires the same kinds of teaching considerations used in other content area instruction.	
	I know of or have a set of procedures and techniques to teach with each of the arts.	
	I do not have time to develop teaching techniques and procedures needed to infuse arts activity into my current/future teaching.	
	Prescribed lesson examples and teaching steps are a good starting point for me to begin teaching with the arts.	
	I learn best from how other K-8 teachers have actually taught arts-infused lessons in their own classrooms.	
	I am comfortable experimenting with a variety of ways to teach with the arts across the curriculum.	

This chapter focuses on considerations for planning and implementing a successful series of instructional events in arts-infused lessons across the curriculum.

After some discussion about planning, you will revisit the teaching sequences and instructional techniques of two of our contributing teachers. Finally, you will have the opportunity to create and review instructional sequences and strategies for your own arts-infused lesson(s)—those built on the purposeful planning stages you have already completed throughout your self-study exercises in this book.

What Are Some Ways to Plan for Instruction With the Arts?

Congratulations. You have already laid most of the groundwork for your arts-infused lesson(s). By now, you know what you want to accomplish and need to organize a personalized sequence of teaching events to effectively reach your purposeful planning goals.

As you do, continue to focus on your own teaching purposes established throughout your self-study processes in this book. That is, *seek to teach K-8 standards-based classroom content and meet student needs through the inclusion of arts activities as a powerful way to teach, learn, do, know, and remember.* Linked to this important purpose is to *increase both your and your students' understanding and knowledge of the arts themselves.*

Refocus on "Big Picture" Ideas: The Arts Content Standards

Classroom instruction involving the arts can be viewed in a *variety* of ways. In order to be true to this book's purpose of increasing understanding and knowledge of the arts themselves, let's first reconsider that important perspective. From a broad-based arts-education (discipline-specific) viewpoint, music, dance, theatre, and visual art instructional activities might include the following types of teaching sequences and opportunities for student learning (California Department of Education, 1996; Music Educators National Conference (MENC), 1994):

Increasing artistic perception: Processing of information about elements found within the arts. An example of this standards-based component is as follows: A teacher displays a painting, photograph, or illustration related to the curriculum theme or topic at hand. He then asks questions related to what students see and guides students to learn to identify and apply new vocabulary (visual art terms) of *foreground, background, subject,* and *horizontal and vertical arrangement.*

5.1 Create Your *Own* Translations of Components of the Arts

The arts-discipline, content standards' components and K–8 classroom examples offered here are a created, composite view of all four arts based on both the National Standards in Arts Education (MENC, 1994) and the *Visual and Performing Arts Framework for California Pubic Schools: Kindergarten Through Grade Twelve* (1996). Therefore, you may need to make translations.

Make your own list of arts components based on the overall or "big picture" language of your own state or district Arts standards. Then create and discuss a direct, tangible classroom example of each with a methods class peer or school-site colleague.

For more information and examples of Arts standards, see Chapter 7, "Unpacking the Arts Standards' Big Ideas."

Creating and performing art. For example, after a whole-class model, a teacher assigns small groups the task of creating and then performing for peers a theatre tableaux (i.e., wordless physical staging) of a scene of historical significance directly related to the history topic at hand. Student scenes are then interpreted, evaluated, and discussed by the entire class as a way to connect the meaning of the tableaux interpretation to the historically significant event.

Analyzing and valuing: Learning to make informed judgments about the arts. For instance, students are to create and perform an original movement sequence based on the formation of different kinds of angles. During the beginning of this geometry/dance lesson, the teacher has modeled and led her students in active experimentation/exploration in the use of space, energy, line, force, expression, and other dance concepts. Students are asked to remember, write about (critique), and form their own opinions of each group's performance, linking appropriate dance vocabulary to the geometry terms and definitions (e.g., acute angle).

Learning about and making connections between the arts within their historical and cultural contexts. For example, a teacher shows a short video clip of the singer/songwriter Woody Guthrie singing his famous song, "This Land Is Your Land." The students learn to sing the song and then learn the history of how Guthrie composed the melody and lyrics during a long 1930s road trip across the United States. They see photo slides of people of that era (i.e., Great Depression), graphics, etc., and make historical connections to the lyrics of the song. They then write and perform their own original verses (set to the melody of "This Land Is Your Land" reflecting current social concerns in the United States.

Comparing and connecting learning with the arts with other subject areas and careers. For example, young students are read an informational book about the metamorphosis of caterpillars to butterflies. First they creatively move to an out-loud, expressive reading of the text of Eric Carle's *The Very Hungry Caterpillar* (1994, Philomel). They are read information and study and discuss the life of the artist, Eric Carle. Later, they watch a short Disney video—an animated version of the book text and illustrations. They then make their own torn paper artwork of the metamorphosis. Finally, they share the "story" of their own artwork out loud (Literacy—Oral Language Development) and demonstrate (through physical movement—Dance) how their imagined (art work) caterpillars moved, cocooned, and emerged as butterflies as the students use the appropriate science terms.

The strength of instructional planning with and through the arts has been well established and discussed throughout this book. The instructional events in the examples above were organized into composite categories based on content components of the arts themselves (per State of California and National Standards in the Arts). (Again, make needed adjustments for your own state and school district standards.)

You should be able to clearly understand how these real-life examples of *other content instruction* were successfully *paired and infused with arts content instruction* (and vice versa). As such, the major purposes of this book once again come to life. Now it's time to discuss how lessons like this were put together and actually taught through attention to carefully chosen instructional sequences of arts-infused lesson events.

Characteristics of Successful Arts-Infused Lessons

We already know that (among other things) *we want our arts-infused lessons to be actively linked to our students' standards-based learning needs.* That is a given. What may be harder to define and implement is an equally strong desire to purposefully create teaching strategies, procedures, and techniques that are *highly engaging, expressive,* and *memorable* for your students. Equally important is whether or not certain teaching sequences are actually *possible* for you to plan and accomplish (given your and your students' time restraints and arts skill levels/experience) during arts-infused activities in your own classroom.

Within the many teacher examples you've already read in this book, and embedded within expert curriculum research about K-8 classroom teachers' use of the arts across the curriculum (e.g., Barrett, 2001; Cornett, 2006b; Gelineau, 2004; Hancock, 2007; Jensen, 2005; Many & Henderson, 2005; McDonald, 2008; McDonald & Fisher, 2002, 2004, 2006; Snyder, 2001; Stake, Bresler, & Mabry, 1991), common characteristics of successful arts-infused lessons emerge. These characteristics may be generally summarized as follows:

- *After purposeful planning, teachers need to be willing to experiment within various arts contexts and activities* to establish their own and their students' comfort zone within arts-infused instruction.
- *Teachers need to plan for materials and establish specific procedures for arts-infused lessons* including sequencing appropriate lesson time frames; equipment/materials (setup, dispensation, usage, and cleanup); room/space considerations; student peer/group dynamics and needs for tracking work progress; and ways to assess (both informally and formally) how content was enriched and made more memorable with and through the arts.

- *Teachers need to actively and enthusiastically model structured examples* of various arts processes and end products they want their students to work toward.

- *Arts-infused lessons need to be activity centered* with focus on *direct participation and expressive engagement of all students* including those with special needs.

- *Children need to actively "do" and "create"* to express their understanding through the arts and make meaning and memory in connection with other subject matter at hand.

- *In addition to large-group instruction, students need opportunities and choices to work alone, in pairs, or in small groups to create and recreate through the arts.* Teachers need to creatively structure and positively reward expectations of progress within individual, partner, and group work so that time is not wasted with off-task behavior and confusion.

- *Student art-making processes and products need to be shared and evaluated with others.* These informal classroom sharing sessions ("gallery" displays, music, dance or theatre performances, etc.) are further avenues for students to learn from peers. Informal and formal displays and performances provide students a *goal* to work toward and make all feel included in that goal.

- *Informal sharing sessions are therefore an important form of assessment.* Informal, authentic assessments also provide a chance for the teacher to reinforce and reconnect to content learning at hand through group discussion, vocabulary and concept review, and possible written assessments. They also provide teachers and students another vehicle for expressing and understanding what was learned with and through the arts.

- *After arts-infused lessons, it is helpful and informative for* both *the teacher and student to reflect on the arts-activity processes.* Through reflection (individually written and/or discussed with others) teachers and students are able to determine what arts-infused processes worked well, what events were most memorable toward the content learning connections at hand, and what may need revision and reconsideration for future arts-infused lessons.

● BEYOND THE CLASSROOM

Read more about Arts within the curriculum: For extensive examples of rationale and research, standards-based lesson/curriculum models, and assessment strategies, see the following excellent sources:

Barrett, J. (2001). Interdisciplinary work and musical integrity. *Music Educators Journal, 87*(5), 27–31.

Burz, H. L., & Marshall, K. (1999). *Performance based curriculum for music and visual arts: From knowing to showing.* Thousand Oaks, CA: Corwin Press.

Cornett, C. (2006). *Creating meaning through literature and* the arts: An integration resource for classroom teachers (3rd ed.). Upper Saddle River, NJ: Prentice Hall.

Gelineau, P. (2004). *Integrating the arts across the elementary school curriculum.* Belmont, CA: Wadsworth.

Hancock, M. (2007). *A celebration of literature and response: Children, books, and teachers in the K–8 classrooms* (2nd ed.). Upper Saddle River, NJ: Prentice Hall.

Jacobs, H. H. (1989). *Interdisciplinary curriculum: Design and implementation.* Alexandria, VA: Association for Supervision and Curriculum Development.

Jacobs, H. H. (1997). *Mapping the big picture: Integrating curriculum and assessment K-12.* Alexandria, VA: Association for Supervision and Curriculum Development.

Jensen, E. (2005). *Arts with the brain in mind* (2nd ed.). Alexandria, VA: Association for Supervision and Curriculum Development.

Many, J., & Henderson, S. (2005). Developing a sense of audience: An examination of one school's instructional contexts. *Reading Horizons, 45*(4), 321–348.

McDonald, N., & Fisher, D. (2002). *Developing arts-loving readers: Top 10 questions teachers are asking about Integrated Arts Education.* Lanham, MD: Scarecrow.

McDonald, N., & Fisher, D. (2006). *Teaching literacy through the arts.* New York: Guilford.

Snyder, S. (2001). Connection, correlation, and integration. *Music Educators Journal, 87*(5), 32–39.

Stake, R., Bresler, L., & Mabry, L., (1991). *Custom and cherishing: The arts in elementary schools.* Urbana: National Arts Education Research at the University of Illinois.

Instructional Components and Sequence in Arts-Infused Lessons

With the above characteristics in mind, what follows is a practical, generalized list of suggested components you may want to consider within your own customized, arts-infused instructional lesson sequence(s).

The following list of lesson components is meant to be food for thought. While some teachers may choose to use all of these components in sequential order, others may choose to use some of the components best suited to their own students, their lesson idea and art(s) involved, planning and teaching time frames, and willingness to experiment with and through the arts.

Introduction/Anticipatory Set

This is a simple "hook-in" activity, display, or media or live event eliciting direct student engagement, participation, a surprise element, or a question.

Key considerations for introductions/anticipatory set are as follows:

- *Keep an introduction short.* Aim for immediate student attention and interest, variety, and links to the topic, goals, and arts-infused activity at hand.

- *Solicit discussion.* Ask probing questions (discussion or written) to cause students to be curious and then identify what they would like to know.
- *Use literacy skills and senses.* Link to the terminology and big ideas within content areas studied. Use vocabulary cards or lists of key words.

Modeling/Use of Materials

These are a group-presented and actively involved, teacher-led example of a short process or an end product. The model is linked to the upcoming arts task, obviously connected to content subject matter at hand.

- Key considerations about modeling and use of materials include the following:
- These are *direct models* (e.g., song or CD recording, actual visual art piece or art-making process, dance sequence (live or video clip), dramatic scene or monologue (live or video clip), etc., serving to *structure* the students' understanding of the upcoming independent, partner, large- or small-group work (task) processes.
- Be sure to *pair the model with appropriate art(s) terms* so that the students learn to identify what they are doing in the arts.

Debrief the Model

This is an instructional technique of using probing questions in large- or small-group discussions to elicit student vocabulary about modeled processes, such as "How were things done?" or "What happened next?" or "What do you think about what happened?" etc.

Key considerations in debriefing arts infused lesson models include:

- The need to incorporate the use of art(s) materials, terms, and concepts *in connection* to other subject area "big idea" concepts and content learning needs at hand. List all terminology and student ideas.

Invitation to Create

This is a direct, *positive invitation* (out loud, written, projected on PowerPoint, etc.) for students to create alone, or in interaction during a *specific task* with a partner or small group, in *active art-making contexts* (e. g., make visual art, create and perform a piece of music, dramatic scene or original movement sequence, write and perform original verses to a song, etc.).

Key components and considerations in an invitation to students to create:

- An *invitation to create* includes your positive enthusiasm and *clearly* stated or posted goals, e.g., "Your (our) goal is to create your own (our own) _____ incorporating the ideas we just discussed and identified."

- Refer students back to the example modeled earlier in the lesson, as original student ideas could form or find their structure in the modeled arts activity (see sidebar).

> **5.2 Encourage Artistic Creativity and Experimentation Within Structure**
>
> Be sure to let students know that their work does not need to be exactly like the model. Encourage students to talk about their own ideas and ways to create the task at hand as they *follow the same structure but do NOT replicate* the exact model. Let them know that artists create their own versions of ideas to express meaning.

Independent Practice: Allow Time to Create

Creativity takes time but needs structure too. Structure time frames (at first these may be wild estimates, so be willing to experiment) to allow students to think, begin, revise, rethink, begin again, and finally, go through their own art-making processes.

Key considerations in independent practice:

- Remember that time frames may need to be fluid, just as the creative act of making or doing arts may fluctuate. Time frames may vastly vary according to the arts activity, student's age and abilities, physical space in your classroom, school schedule, student's experience with the arts, and your own experience with leading arts processes.

- *Sequential lessons* (spread over a few days' or more lesson sequences) may allow important additional opportunities to review and connect content, vocabulary, and memory of the arts-infused learning at hand. *Consider spreading arts-infused lesson content over time.*

  - For instance, a *visual art project* may be begun (lay out pencil drawings, decisions made on color choices, etc.) on one day and added to during subsequent, sequential lessons.

  - In *musical contexts*, after singing a song together on one day, your students might work in groups to learn new verses to the song the next day, create and sing original verses on another day, and finally create and perform movements to those original verses on the third day.

  - In *theatre* contexts, your students might first discuss and jot down their original scene's story line (in short phrases used in an outline) and on the next day get "on their feet" to create and stage dialogue, character action, and movement.

Teacher as Facilitator of Creativity Processes

Many classroom teachers serve as *facilitators* during their student's individual, partner, or small-group arts making experiences.

Key considerations here are:

- Teacher roles of "leader and modeler" and "up-front classroom leadership" can naturally shift during arts-making processes.

- During independent work, teachers find themselves primarily *coaching*, clarifying information, procedures, and ideas, and motivating (cheerleading) student efforts to allow them to express, discover, invent, experiment, and most important, *succeed* on their own within the structured arts-making process.

- *Teachers report success that the simple assignment of student leadership roles within each small group can really save time!* For example, a "scribe" is a student who records group ideas and formats, the "reporter" communicates information and questions/answers to the teacher and back to the group, and the "director" helps guide the group in disputes and final decisions.

   You might want to also assign a "time manager" in each group who reminds others about how much time they have to complete various stages of the arts-making processes. Even younger students love to serve in these roles.

- *To build a broad base of student leadership and peer interactions in your class, make sure the same students are not always with the same partners or small groups or in the same leadership roles within their groups.* Also, older students may choose to elect or volunteer to serve in certain roles within a cooperative group. Some teachers keep a card file on each student and assign certain roles and responsibilities on a rotating basis.

- *Be sure to visit each group or pair of partners many times during their creative work.* Be prepared to frequently reclarify instructions and remodel arts processes, etc. As we know, students tend to ask more questions when engaged in small groups.

- *Within sequential lesson formats over different days, consider a system of "progress checks"* or simple written descriptions of what the group has accomplished so far. Be sure the students know that these "progress checks" are part of their grade on the project, performance evaluation, etc.

Informal Performance/Displays (Authentic Assessments) and Other Forms of Evaluations

Informal classroom displays, presentations, and/or performances are a rich opportunities for students and the teacher to see each other's work.

Key considerations here are:

- *Sharing opportunities provide important goals to motivate and structure students' creative efforts.*
- *Structure for success.* Be sure each individual, pair of partners, or small group gets *equal* time and space to share their efforts with others.
- *Create and share criteria for students to evaluate their own and other's efforts* through the use of written rubrics or short, structured oral critiques or discussion.
- *Allow each group to present their work and ask a probing question of the larger group.* Rather than ask the class to answer their created question, *allow the presenting group (partner, individual, etc.) to answer their own question* after giving the large group some time to think about that question. Then the whole class can offer their ideas about the question at hand (another way to elicit student participation).
  - For example, after a dramatic pantomime movement sequence of the "Chain of Infection" (Science content: spread of a virus or bacterial infection), the presentation group could pose the question, "What could Ariel (one of the characters) have done to stop the Chain of Infection?"
- *During class sharing, peers serve as an informed audience* as they think and talk about what was accomplished, and, at the same time, establish further *meaningful connections* to the subject matter at hand. Sharing allows students to see and hear how their peers interpreted the same task, thereby deepening their own interest and meaningful memory of the learning at hand.
- *After a variety of successful informal classroom sharing events, students may be ready to be lead in the preparation of more formal arts-based displays, performances, galleries, etc.* These important events (for other grade-level classes, schoolwide, or for parents and community) can serve to inform and unify colleagues, parents, administrators, and community in the importance of arts within the general curriculum.

Reflection: Students and Teacher

Experience teaches. Both students and teachers have reported that it is useful and educative to reflect upon arts-infused lessons through writing, large-group discussions, checklists, etc.

Key considerations:

- One goal of purposeful reflection activity is to carefully consider and express how the arts activity connected the students to the content learning at hand.

- Another equally important goal is to give the students and the teacher an opportunity to think about and express what they were excited about and enjoyed, felt, found helpful, needed improvement or clarification on, etc., during the arts-infused lesson.

- In these and other ways, self and group reflection can serve as important experiential information to recycle back into improved purposeful planning stages for future arts-infused learning activities.

Arts-Infused Teaching Strategies at Work in the K–8 Classroom

Now that you have considered a number of characteristics and components for instructional sequences in your own lesson(s), let's turn once again to real-life examples from our contributing teachers. What follows are a series of teaching and learning events documented by two of our contributing teachers— one primary and one upper-grade lesson example you have been reading about throughout this book.

> **5.3** **Purposeful planning for lessons can change and evolve over time:**
>
> Note that what two teacher contributors' lesson sequences and content actually taught may have changed somewhat since their initial purposeful planning stages. You can expect the same as you progress from lesson planning to implementation in your own classroom.

K/1 Lesson Instructional Sequence: Ms. Tanonis

As you may remember, one of Rose Tanonis's K/1 lessons was "Integrating Science and the Arts: 'Lifecycle of Butterflies'" (content areas: Science, English Language Arts [Reading/ Author Study, Oral Language], Arts [Visual Art]. (See Figure 5.1, "Ms. Tanonis's Instructional Sequence" for a summary of her chosen instructional sequence and materials used.)

Note that Ms. Tanonis' actual instruction varies a bit from her original plan and focuses instead on the parts of an insect's body. Students created their own "Eric Carle–inspired" painted paper to use within their collage and language arts/ oral language lesson about insect body parts. This early art lesson for K-1 English language and special learners expanded on their recently obtained knowledge and vocabulary about the color wheel through hands-on experimentation with collage technique and overlaying/ blending of color. One accommodation Ms. Tanonis initiated was the use of (insect-body-shaped) templates to provide her students more immediate, tangible, and experiential opportunities to associate, understand, and develop completely new English language vocabulary about those shapes.

When asked to document/describe her step-by-step instructional sequences during this arts-infused lesson (the prompt on the contributing teachers' self-study was "What happened?"), Ms. Tanonis provided the following rich description:

5.4 Arts-infused Instruction can be highly individualized:

As you read, think about the various stages of Ms. Tanonis' instruction discussed earlier in this chapter, i.e. "anticipatory set, modeling, independent work", etc., written in italics throughout her narrative descriptions. Notice the flow of her instructional sequence here, rather than a strict adherence to a formula of prescribed lesson steps.

> I read to the class *The Very Hungry Caterpillar* by Eric Carle *(Introduction/Anticipatory set)*. I pointed out the beautiful artwork and showed them that paper has texture from brushstrokes, fingers, sponges, sticks, etc.
>
> After the story, I put out 9" × 12" pieces of white construction paper on each student's desk. Then I poured red, orange, yellow, green, blue, purple, pink, brown, white, and black tempera paint into small plastic cups *(Materials Set Up, Modeling,* and *Invitation to Create)*. It did not matter what colors were used or who got what color. I told the children that the paper we make will be used by everyone. No one has ownership of the paper and no names would be written on the paper.
>
> I grouped the children in pairs. Each child painted their whole white sheet with the color they were given *(Independent Practice: Create)*. When we could not see any white coming through, they switched colors with their neighbor.
>
> *(Teacher as Facilitator)* They were encouraged to use fingers, brushes, ends of brushes, marbles rolled in the new color, sticks, whatever to add texture to their paper. Even spackle like Jackson Pollock! (You can do this one or have the children switch with another student for another color to add more texture. I let these dry overnight.)
>
> *(Sequential Lesson Development)* Then I made templates *(Accommodation for Students)* of the insects used in the four Eric Carle stories *(The Very Grouchy Ladybug* [1996], *The Very Lonely Firefly* [1995], *The Very Hungry Caterpillar* [1994], *The Very Quiet Cricket* [1990]) out of card stock or heavy, thick paper.
>
> I picked 5 students for each story to make the insects (after reading each book and on sequential days). As we traced the template pieces onto the backside of the painted paper, we discussed the parts of the insect: head, thorax, abdomen, wings, eyes, antennae, and six legs need to be present in order to be an insect.
>
> We traced and cut out all the parts. Then the children glued them onto black paper and assembled their insect. With black and white crayon they drew on the eyes, antennae, and legs.
>
> After the out loud reading of each of the 4 Carle books, I picked 5 different students until I had 5 butterflies, 5 ladybugs, 5 fireflies, and 5 crickets.
>
> Then I put them on the wall to display *(Informal Display/ Sharing)*. We wrote afterwards about our insects and what was needed to make them a real insect *(Reflection)*.

FIGURE 5.1   Ms. Tanonis's Instructional Sequence: (K/1) Integrating Science
and Language Arts With Visual Art and Dance: "Parts of an Insect"

Introduction/Anticipatory Set

- Out-loud reading of Eric Carle's book(s) (see "Materials" below)
- Pointed out visual art qualities in Carle's art work

Materials Used

- Four books by Eric Carle: *The Very Grouchy Ladybug* (1996), *The Very Lonely Firefly* (1995), *The Very Hungry Caterpillar* (1994), *The Very Quiet Cricket* (1990).
- 9" × 12" white construction paper and black paper
- 8½" × 11" card stock or heavy paper
- Tempera paint of many colors
- Paint brushes, newspaper, marbles, glue, scissors, plastic cups

Modeling/Invitation to Create

- Invitation to create Eric Carle–inspired colored paper to be used by everyone later in the insect project.
- It did not matter what colors were used or who got what color. No ownership of the paper and no names would be written on the paper.
- Later, students used class-created paper to make a variety of insect parts of 4 different insects (groups of 5 students).

Independent Practice

- Students grouped in pairs to paint the white paper with the colors they were given
- 9" × 12" pieces of white construction paper on each student's desk. Red, orange, yellow, green, blue, purple, pink, brown, white, and black tempera paint in small plastic cups.
- When no white space could be seen, students switched colors with their neighbor.
- Later (Sequential Lessons), 5 students picked to construct each of the 4 types of insects using class created painted paper: 5 butterflies, 5 ladybugs, 5 fireflies, and 5 crickets.
- Students and teacher traced (Accommodation) and cut out all the insect parts.
- Children glued them onto black paper and assembled their insect. With black and white crayon they drew on the eyes, antennae, and legs.
- During independent work, students and teacher discussed the parts of the insect: Head, thorax, abdomen, wings, eyes, antennae, and six legs need to be present in order to be an insect.

Teacher as Facilitator

- Worked along with students while frequently using visual art and science vocabulary.
- Encouraged student experimentation in painting techniques and devices to create texture.

Forms of Assessment/Evaluation

- Discussion with individuals and groups during art making.
- Informal classroom art display (Gallery of Insects)
- Students wrote about art-making processes involving insect parts.
- Dance/Movement: Students demonstrated knowledge of insect parts through movement sequences paired with oral language descriptions of insect parts

Reflection

- Students: Discussion, writing, viewing others' art pieces, oral language, and vocabulary in visual art and science.
- Teacher: Written reflection about what students learned about insects through visual art and movement activity.

Ms. Tanonis goes on to reflect about how she was able to assess or evaluate
student learning linked to the "big ideas" her students needed to know during this

Ms. Tanonis's K/1 students proudly display a gallery of "Insect Artwork".

Photo by Rose Tanonis.

arts-infused Science content lesson. Notice how she utilized both oral language and movement (Arts) within her assessment. Ms. Tanonis continued,

> After they made their artwork, they showed me the parts necessary to make an insect an insect. I taught them to point to their head and say "head," point to their eyes and say "eyes," point their index fingers out of the tops of their heads and say, "antennae," cross their hands over their chest and say "thorax," put their hands together and pull them down to their hipbones and say, "abdomen", and lastly hold up 6 fingers and say, "6 legs."
>
> They had to do this independently, so I knew they got it. The movement activity helped the kids learn thorax and abdomen. Even if the student could not say the part to me, they could show me they understood what they needed to see to determine if it was truly an insect. *The vocabulary became visual!*
>
> I love the way they turned out. Even using the templates, the insects have personality because of the hand drawn eyes, antennae, and legs. Each is unique depending on the paper the child chose.

When asked what she might have *done differently to improve* her arts-infused lesson *(Reflection)*, Ms. Tanonis offered this practical advice to herself and others who work with primary students:

> Make sure that the plastic cups are sturdy and easy for your students to hold. The ones I used did not tip over even with a large paintbrush left inside. Do not fill the cups beyond half way! Use the tops of boxes from the Xerox paper boxes, for the children to work inside of, as well as newspaper on all the tables.
>
> Also, in hindsight, I would have made my templates of each insect that has a thorax. Only the ladybug and cricket have thoraxes! The rest have eyes, antennae, wings, legs, and heads. I would redesign the insects so the lesson would be more powerful.

Sixth-Grade Math Instructional Sequence: Ms. Elemont

As you may remember, one of Christi Elemont's sixth-grade math lessons was "Integrating Math and the Arts: 'Measuring and Classifying Angles and Transforma-

Ms. Elemont's students are thinking, "Who knew measuring and classifying angles was so much fun . . . and so healthy?

Photo by Christi Elemont.

tions'" (content areas: Math [Geometry] and Dance). Ms. Elemont titles this activity "Geometry Aerobics." (As you read, *notice that her arts-infused lesson is a teacher-created, large-group modeled, practiced, and performed, whole-class activity, not a small-group process.*)

When asked to document/describe her step-by-step instructional sequences for this lesson (with the prompt "What happened?"), Ms. Elemont provided the following enthusiastic and candid descriptions (see summary in Figure 5.2):

5.5 Arts-Infused lessons can feature many forms of instruction.

As you read and think about the various instructional stages of Ms. Elemont's math with dance activity, notice again that the lesson components (i.e. "Anticipatory Set, Invitation to Create, Modeling, Teacher as Facilitator", etc.) are again placed *in italics* throughout her narrative description. As you read, also keep in mind that Ms. Elemont uses her *own created dance model* to provide a *direct example* of the whole group dance lesson activity ("Geometry Aerobics") *her students are to master.* (See Figure 5.2: "Ms. Elemont's Instructional Sequence")

1. Once students have knowledge of the content (angles), it is time to start "Geometry Aerobics"! *(Introduction Anticipatory Set/ Invitation to Create)*

2. First, I created a short simple dance on my own and demonstrated and taught it to my students *(Lesson Modeling)*. Example of a movement sequence: 90 degrees, 45 degrees, straight angle, translation, 360 degree rotation.

3. I put the steps on the docucam and showed the students the simple created dance.

4. *(Whole Group Arts Activity with Independent Practice)* Next, I acted like an aerobics instructor and showed the students how to do each movement (teach in pieces). Then, we put it all together. (It is important to go piece by piece and show the students what each move should look like.)

5. I helped them individually by walking around as the class practiced a particular move *(Teacher as Facilitator)*.

6. Once the class knows the dance by heart and everyone does it 100%, have them create their own dance *(Independent Practice)*. Practice and perform for another class *(Authentic Assessment: Performance Sharing)*.

Ms. Elemont continued to describe what she observed during her arts-infused activity *(Reflection)*:

At first, I noticed a few students were very shy and weren't sure if they wanted to participate in the dance (typical middle school behavior) even though I have established a very low-stress environment in my classroom. Once students saw everyone's enthusiasm and everyone else trying it, they joined in.

The students love when I walk around and really motivate them just as an aerobics instructor does *(Teacher as Facilitator)*. They really try their best at the dancing and

FIGURE 5.2 Ms. Elemont's Instructional Sequence: Integrating Math and the Arts: "Measuring and Classifying Angles and Transformations: Geometry Aerobics". Content Areas: Math (Geometry), and Dance

Introduction/Anticipatory Set
- Verbal surprise: "Now that we know the basics, it's time for Geometry Aerobics!
- Teacher performs an original, whole-body dance movement sequence directly linked to math content (Geometry—Classifying Angles and Transformations).

Materials Used
- Teacher determines space needs. Students push in chairs and use space behind table desks.
- State-adopted text in Mathematics (dance based on math terminology and concepts from standards' based math text).
- Teacher's original choreography and notes (for class docucam projection to help guide the teaching of the dance sequence).
- Recorded music—Popular dance music appropriate for use in the classroom.

Modeling/Invitation to Create
- Teacher model of dance.
- Projection of steps to the dance tied to angle formation and transformations.
- Students practiced slowly guided by teacher models of each step of the dance.
- Angles and transformations terminology used (linked) out loud by students as they learn the parts of the dance sequence.

Independent Practice
- Students continue to independently practice the group dance steps by viewing the projected choreography and experimenting slowly on their own.

- Whole-group practice (with recorded music) with and without the teacher over many days
- Once students master the group dance, assign task of creating their own dance to teach to the whole group.

Teacher as Facilitator
- After initial group instruction, teacher roams the room to help students physically master the dance pattern.
- Individual coaching to clarify direction, use of space, transitions between movements, and math terminology.

Forms of Assessment/Evaluation
- Authentic: Performance of the group dance
- Students reference understanding gained through "Geometry Aerobics" within formal assessments: quizzes, journal entries, leadership of class in "warm-ups," multiple-choice test on geometry terms.
- Teacher determines increased memory of learning at hand, improved test scores, evidence (written and oral) of students' accessing dance experience to make meaning of geometry terms and concepts.

Reflection
- Students: Discussion, writing, viewing, and critique of whole-class dance and personal participation, positive memory of experiences, request for more dance activity.
- Teacher: Written reflection, concluded that more dance activity was needed (both whole-class and small-group original choreography).

the challenge is to get them all in unison but eventually it does happen. It just takes practice everyday. *(Group Practice/Rehearsal)*

I noticed that if you don't hold students accountable for the moves, they don't give it their all. It is very important to be enthusiastic and energetic while doing this lesson.

When asked about how she *assessed/evaluated* student learning after this arts in-fused math (geometry) lesson, Ms. Elemont starts by reminding us of her standards-based math content "big ideas." These include:

Classify Angles: Acute, Right, Obtuse, Straight

Measuring Angles: Knowing what a specific angle looks like.

Transformations: Reflections, Rotations and Translations

To assess student learning of these big ideas in math, Ms. Elemont uses the fol-lowing (*Formal and Authentic Assessment/Evaluation*) to help determine the affect (memorable learning of math concepts) of this arts-infused lesson experience:

1. Quizzes: Students are given a weekly quiz were they are asked to measure and classify angles, as well as depict and create transformations.
2. Journals: Students complete a warm-up at the beginning of each class to rein-force previously learned concepts. They are randomly chosen by popsicle sticks to come up to the front and explain a problem to the class. However, they can use their "phone a friend" (used in TV quiz shows) option to help if they get stuck.
3. Unit Assessment: Multiple-choice test on Geometry.

When asked about *how the arts-infused lesson activity contributed to student under-standing of math concepts (Assessment/Evaluation)*, Ms. Elemont explains,

Even though the students weren't using a protractor to physically measure the angles, they did even better by showing the angles with their hands so they really knew what the angle should look like. Also, when I would ask them to show me a "translation," they would think back to the aerobics and say, "Oh, that's a slide!" and that helped them remember what a translations should look like. Also, I could tell from their quiz results that they were grasping and owning the information. They did very well on the tasks I asked them to do.

After the unit was over (*Student Reflection*), one student commented, "Can we make up a dance to this new chapter so I can get a good grade?" Another said, "This is my favorite thing to do in math class and I did the best I have ever done on my test!" Another student added, "I didn't realize how much I knew about angles until I got my test back."

Finally, Ms. Elemont reflected upon her lesson and future teaching by adding (*Teacher Reflection*),

I would like for my students to create their own geometry aerobic dances and have them get in small groups and teach them to each other. Then, they could vote on whose dance they like the best and have them teach it to the class. (*Shared leadership-Performance*).

In conclusion, Ms. Elemont reflected,

> My students were very enthusiastic and loved learning through dancing. I saw constant smiles throughout the whole process. I was smiling also when I saw their assessment grades. I will definitely incorporate this into my lessons for years to come . . . it will get better and better each year. My new challenge for myself is to create dances to other mathematics topics. We will see.

Conclusion

This chapter defined and outlined certain characteristics and components of arts-infused instruction to consider in your own purposeful planning and teaching. Two of our teacher contributors (Ms. Tanonis and Ms. Elemont) provided real-life examples of these instructional components in action. There you saw evidence of teacher creativity, originality, and flexibility as they experimented and reflected upon their classroom learning and assessment activities.

You undoubtedly concluded that arts-activity infusion does closely follow the same kinds of guidelines found within *all* quality content instruction in the general curriculum. *That is, teachers should plan lesson events to immediately engage student interest and participation in the learning at hand.* And, once that student interest and engagement is established, direct modeling with invitations to create and do can flow seamlessly into structured, sequenced student projects (individual, pairs, small groups) or whole-group experiences designed to accomplish the arts-infused task at hand. Finally, assessment/evaluation and student/teacher reflections of the arts activity can take many forms; these will be further discussed in Chapter 6.

Self-Study

Mapping Your Arts-Infused Instructional Sequence

Instructions for Using Figure 5.3

It's now time to complete the following reflective activities both *before and then after teaching your lesson(s)* in lab groups in your methods class, in field experiences, or in own classroom.

The directions on Figure 5.3, "Self-Study: Mapping Your Arts-Infused Instructional Sequence," will clarify which parts of the form should be filled in before and which after your teaching. Similar to activities in previous chapters, this form should be completed by using the following sequence of activities:

- Before a discussion with a peer, use the "agree/disagree" statements you answered in the Focus Activity at the very beginning of this chapter. (If you did not respond to the statements *before* you read this chapter, do so now *in the "after" column*, and a discussion can still work.)

- *Discuss* your answers to this chapter's Focus Activity with a class peer or school-site colleague (by phone, online, or in person). Make mental notes of how you and your peers answered these anticipatory prompts.

- *Revisit* your own purposeful plan(s) recorded within your Self-Study forms from Chapters 2 through 4. Be prepared to realize that your plans may have evolved and changed a bit by now.

- *Complete* the first part only of *Figure 5.3, "Self-Study: Mapping Your Arts-Infused Instructional Sequence"* (a rough draft before you teach your arts-infused lesson).

- *Dialogue with methods class peer(s) or school-site colleague* about your instructional plan *before* you teach your lesson. *Revise* if needed.

- *Teach* your arts-infused lesson(s).

- Within 12 to 24 hours after teaching, *complete the bottom portion of the form in Figure 5.3.*

- *Read/discuss your completed Figure 5.3 Self-Study,* Dialogue with a peer or small group of peers in your methods class or at your school site. (Completed forms could easily be shared online.)

- *Optional: Create an original format of the Self-Study form* (Figure 5.3) *as needed:* Create your own forms linked to what *you* need in your own classroom. Share a customized version of the Self-Study form with your methods class or school-site colleagues.

- *Keep your complete form (Figure 5.3) on computer or in a hard copy file* to document, store, and share your purposeful plan(s).

FIGURE 5.3 Self-Study: "Mapping Your Arts-Infused Instructional Sequence"

Instructions: This self-study has 2 sections. Fill in the first section before you teach your arts-infused lesson(s). The second section should be completed after you teach.

Name: _____   Date: _____

Methods Class/Grade/Subject: _____

School Site: _____

Topic or Arts-Infused Lesson(s) Theme: _____

Content Area(s): _____

"Big Ideas": _____

State Content Standards: _____

Art or arts you plan to use: _____ _____ _____ _____

State Arts Content Standards: _____

Briefly list (abbreviated outline format) your ideas for the following instructional components:

Introduction/Anticipatory Set:

Modeling/Use of Materials/Debrief the Model:

Materials Used:

Invitation to Create:

Independent Practice:

Teacher as Facilitator:

Informal Performance Sharing or Display/Assessment:

AFTER teaching this lesson, fill in the following:

What happened? Briefly outline lesson events in order of how they *actually happened* in your classroom.

List ALL materials used:

What kinds of things did you observe during the processes of this lesson?

How did you evaluate/assess student learning linked to the "big ideas" your students needed to know? How do you know they understood these big ideas? (Refer to your previous self-study forms from Chapters 2–4).

In your personal opinion, *how* did your use of arts activity contribute to student understanding in this lesson?

In hindsight, what would you do differently during this lesson?

What are your personal thoughts about *how* this classroom experience might shape your own future lesson planning?

References

Barrett, J. (2001). Interdisciplinary work and musical integrity. *Music Educators Journal, 87*(5), 27–31.

Burz, H. L., & Marshall, K. (1999). *Performance based curriculum for music and visual arts: From knowing to showing.* Thousand Oaks, CA: Corwin Press.

Carle, E. (1994). *The very hungry caterpillar.* New York: Philomel.

Carle, E. (1990). *The very quiet cricket.* New York: Philomel.

Carle, E. (1995). *The very lonely firefly.* New York: Philomel.

Carle, E. (1996). *The very grouchy ladybug.* New York: HarperCollins.

California Department of Education. (1996). *Visual and performing arts framework for California public schools: Kindergarten through grade twelve.* Sacramento: California Department of Education.

Cornett, C. (2006a). Center stage: Arts-based read-alouds. *The Reading Teacher, 60*(3), 234–240.

Cornett, C. (2006b). *Creating meaning through literature and the arts: An integration resource for classroom teachers* (3rd ed.). Upper Saddle River, NJ: Merrill/Prentice Hall.

Gelineau, P. (2004). *Integrating the arts across the elementary school curriculum.* Belmont CA: Wadsworth.

Hancock, M. (2007). *A celebration of literature and response: Children, books, and teachers in K-8 classrooms* (2nd ed.). Upper Saddle River, NJ: Prentice Hall.

Jacobs, H. H. (1989). *Interdisciplinary curriculum: Design and implementation.* Alexandria, VA: Association for Supervision and Curriculum Development.

Jacobs, H. H. (1997). *Mapping the big picture: Integrating curriculum and assessment K–12.* Alexandria, VA: Association for Supervision and Curriculum Development.

Jensen, E. (2005). *Arts with the brain in mind* (2nd ed.). Alexandria, VA: Association for Supervision and Curriculum Development.

Many, J., & Henderson, S. (2005). Developing a sense of audience: An examination of one school's instructional contexts. *Reading Horizons, 45*(4), 321–348.

McDonald, N. (2008). Standards in the arts and arts within literacy instruction." In J. Flood, S. Brice-Heath, & D. Lapp (Eds.), *The Handbook of Research on Teaching Literacy Through the Communicative, Performing, and Visual Arts Volume II: Sponsored by the International Reading Association* (pp. 567–572). Mahwah, NJ: Lawrence Erlbaum.

McDonald, N., & Fisher, D. (2002). *Developing arts-loving readers: Top ten questions teachers are asking about integrated arts education.* Lanham, MD: Rowman & Littlefield Education.

McDonald, N., & Fisher, D. (2004). Stormy weather: Leading purposeful curriculum integration with the through the arts." *Teaching Artist Journal, 2*(4), 240–248.

McDonald, N., & Fisher, D. (2006). *Teaching literacy through the arts.* New York: Guilford.

Music Educators National Conference (1994). *Dance, music, theatre, visual arts: What every young American should know and be able to do in the arts: National standards for arts education.* Reston, VA: Music Educators National Conference.

Snyder, S. (2001). Connection, correlation, and integration. *Music Educators Journal, 87*(5), 32–39.

Stake, R., Bresler, L., & Mabry, L. (1991). *Custom and cherishing: The arts in elementary schools.* Urbana: National Arts Education Research Center at the University of Illinois.

Evaluation

[My] students needed to integrate their understanding of land forms, habitats and ecosystems in order to create something original. The medium (open air sketching and water color) allowed for students to express their understanding. Each piece was an individual assessment.

—Mrs. Kate Gray, Grade 3 Contributing Teacher

Directions: Please fill out before and after reading this chapter.

Before Reading Chapter A = agree D = disagree	Statements	After Reading Chapter A = agree D = disagree
	Arts-infused activities should be free from the assessment/evaluation pressure teachers face in other content area instruction	
	Arts-activity infusion requires the same kinds of assessment/evaluation considerations used in other content area instruction.	
	I have/know a set of procedures and techniques to assess and evaluate arts-infused learning activities and student end products.	
	I do not have time to develop additional techniques and procedures needed to evaluate student learning with and through the arts.	

By now you have taught your purposely planned, arts-infused lesson(s). In them, you and your methods class peers or young students undoubtedly engaged in rewarding, memorable, and productive learning activities. Through the self-study exercises at the end of Chapter 5 you have already begun to evaluate and reflect upon your lesson experiences and the learning involved. This chapter is designed to continue and deepen that path of evaluation and assessment linked to arts-infused learning across the curriculum.

After considering several forms of assessment tied to arts-infused learning, you will revisit our contributing teachers' lessons for tangible examples of assessments in action. Finally, you will have the opportunity to further evaluate and reflect upon student understanding in your own lesson(s) and develop a variety of ideas for future assessments of arts-infused learning in your future or current classroom.

Evaluation and Assessment During Arts-Infused lessons

Remember that one goal of this book is for you to purposely plan, create, and teach selected K–8 classroom content through the inclusion of arts activities as a powerful way to teach, learn, do, know, and remember. Here, an additional consideration is needed. That is, to design purposeful assessments to determine what and how your students learned, made meaning, and gained understanding of standards-based, content "big ideas" with and through arts-infused activities. (And, as you do so, recall that another goal is to assess your own and your students' understanding and knowledge of the arts themselves.)

Purposeful planning with the arts involves what Wiggins and McTighe (2006) describe as a *circular* form of curriculum design. McDonald and Fisher (2002) comment,

> Evaluation and assessment (the word *assessment* originally meant to sit beside, as in acts of reflection and dialogue with others) is a natural and cyclical activity designed to improve instruction, learning, and a student's sense of self-efficacy through continuous reflections, discussion, judgment, reevaluation, and experimentation with new learning. The role of the teacher is to ask important questions, encourage student's self-assessment through reflection activity and informed judgment, and provide feedback to the learner (and among learners) toward the improvement and encouragement of their creative and artistic efforts (p. 165).

In terms of your own teaching, the reading and constructive planning stages you already accomplished during the first five chapters of this book will now serve as a cyclical springboard toward your future assessment planning. *This self-constructed information is the platform for understanding how assessments might be naturally embedded within arts-infused learning activities.* Seen in this natural light, *assessments can also be a purposeful outgrowth of those arts-infused activities.* Above all, *assessments can be an evaluative opportunity for both you and your students to determine how arts-infused learning activities augmented and reinforced student understanding of the big ideas you intended to teach.*

Understanding

In addition to *knowledge and skill* about a set of facts and/or procedures and events concerning an instructional topic (big ideas), you also want students *to understand* what they have learned. As you remember, *understanding* implies transfer or application to new situations and contexts, a broader sense of making meaning of what is learned (Wiggins & McTighe, 2006). This ability to transfer knowledge and skill effectively involves the capacity to take what we know and use it creatively, flexibly, and fluently, in different settings or problems, on our own.

So, when your students created or participated in arts-infused activities in your lesson(s), they were undoubtedly involved in *active synthesis and transference of their knowledge into understanding.* Remember that transferability is not mere plugging in of previously learned knowledge and skill. To this, Wiggins and McTighe (2006) explain,

> Note again that the word *understand(ing)* has a verb meaning and a noun meaning. *To understand* a topic or subject is to be able to use (or "apply," in Bloom's sense) knowledge and skill wisely and effectively. *An understanding* is the successful result of trying to understand—the resultant grasp of an unobvious idea, an inference that makes meaning of many discrete (and perhaps seemingly insignificant) elements of knowledge. (p. 43)

Understanding is therefore about *going beyond the information given* (Bruner, 1957/1973). Through arts-infused learning, our students might be able to go beyond, experiment with their skills to obtain new knowledge and "arrive at further understandings if (they) have learned with understanding some key ideas and strategies" (Wiggins & McTighe, 2006, p. 40).

In your own lesson(s), students may have bridged some gaps between what they already knew and needed to know within new situations designed to apply this knowledge. Their meaning making and understanding of intended knowledge and skills was undoubtedly augmented and solidified through their arts-infused activity. These are important concepts to keep in mind as we continue our purposeful planning discussion of arts-infused lesson assessments for classroom use.

Active Assessments to Determine Student Understanding

All good teaching includes many forms of active assessment (e.g., formal and informal, authentic) before, during, and after a lesson (McDonald & Fisher, 2002, 2006). They are checkpoints for understanding. Assessments can be purposely designed to inform the teacher of where students are in their processes of understanding throughout the arts-infused learning tasks.

As you already know from your own teaching experiences, assessments of all kinds can also drive the quality of instruction *during* a lesson. As you check for student understanding through discussion, surveys, writing, small-group facilitation, student products, works, and performances, that information informs you of what to do next and can provide brand-new directions within the course of your lesson experiences. In these ways, active assessments before, during, and after arts-infused lesson experiences also inform you about how that teaching and learning is going and what may need changing in future lessons.

Viewed simply, *assessments can determine if, how, and to what degree your students have learned what you have taught. Evaluations* are forms of assessment that may include a more qualitative response from the learners and a comprehensive interpretation of that learning from the teacher. What follows is a list and discussion of some types of assessments and evaluations you may wish to consider for your arts-infused lessons:

● BEYOND THE CLASSROOM

Be an Assessment Detective

Ask methods class and school-site peers *how* they assess arts-infused activity in their classroom. Identify and keep a list of those assessment tools and procedures that are most linked to your purposeful planning in this book. Look for assessments that are

- Not time-consuming (you can imagine actually doing them in your classroom before, during, and/or after arts-infused activities.)
- Linked to standards-based big ideas in content areas
- Linked to the art(s) standards used within your lesson(s)
- Appropriate to age and ability level of your students
- Use a variety of active assessment tools (written, rubrics, discussion, checklists, reflections, performances, displays, critiques, etc.)

Authentic Assessments

As you know, most of your arts-infused lessons may not result in traditional, formalized arts performances or exhibitions. That is not necessarily the intent or purpose of our purposeful planning here. Not all activity in the arts has to include "rehearsals" and/or a goal of a formalized presentation, performance, or exhibition.

However, the very act of student participation and learning as a student artist (musician, actor, dancer) naturally involves sharing those processes with others and making meaning of that art, as well as the artwork, music, theatre, or dance-infused project itself. These informal and formal opportunities to "show" what the students have learned (*authentic assessments*) "can take place in a variety of ways, every day within our own classrooms" (McDonald & Fisher, 2002, p. 162).

Burz and Marshall (1999) in *Performance-Based Curriculum for Music and the Visual Arts: From Knowing to Showing*, summarize that there are specific learning actions within any art-based project or task. One of these, "production," is characterized by how individuals or groups have experimented or considered many options toward the goal of an informal or formal mini-performance or some kind of display of their project.

In *production* (this book's term is "independent practice"), students are immersed in a learning-action mode. Here, connections and translations of knowledge have been experimented with, discussed and evaluated, incorporated, and applied toward a specific end-product goal (an artwork, sharing of a song, scene, etc.) as representation of the larger learning at hand.

Much has to be considered and worked out in these authentic-assessment-related processes. Students ask others and themselves (sometimes tacitly) important questions about the knowledge-based learning processes in which they are engaged. These include questions and answers about the best way to make, present, move, construct, and/or say things, to show what they have learned.

These kinds of *process* questions and answers (and their subsequent revisions and evaluations) actively propel students toward a more complete *understanding* of the arts-infused learning at hand. "The overall goal here is for the teacher to design ways for the learners to engage in continuous self and group evaluation on a day-by-day basis so that evaluation of arts learning becomes as natural an activity as the creative processes of making that art" (McDonald & Fisher, 2002, p. 165). *This is the essence of learning by doing with and through the arts.*

There are additional learning bonuses for students as they participate in varying types of mini-performances and informal sharing of arts-infused activities. In these authentic and active contexts,

> (in which performance art involves an interested audience), learners become highly motivated to show and demonstrate what they have actively learned and created within particular performance settings. The nature of performance motivation should not be underestimated as a powerful learning tool within integrated arts curriculum in the music, dance, and theatre infused projects. (McDonald & Fisher, 2002, p. 164)

What follows is a list of forms of active, authentic assessments ideas for your consideration and future planning.

Assessment/Evaluation Examples

In-Class Performance Sharing

These are informal opportunities for students to share arts-based projects, performances, demonstrations, artworks, etc.

- Example: Students (and teacher) use a rubric or checklist to evaluate their own and other's efforts. Discussion follows. (See Figure 6.1, "Arts Activity Critique.")

Knowledge Charts/K-W-L

Knowledge Charts, or "K-W-L," are checklists used as both anticipatory and then summative indicators (much like the exercises at the beginning of each chapter of this book) to assess student understanding of "big idea" content within arts-infused activity (Ogle 1986).

- Example: Students fill out a checklist within columns entitled, "What I Think It Means," "What It Really Means," and "Where I Found Out." (See Table 6.1, "Let's Find Out About Strings (Vocabulary Chart).")

FIGURE 6.1 Arts Activity Critique

On a scale of 1 to 5 (5 being the best), rate the following:

Script and story line: _____

Actors: _____

Action: _____

Scenery: _____

Costumes: _____

Props: _____

Overall, I would rate this audience experience experience as a _____ because _____

_____

_____

_____

Note: Example of a 1–5 rating system to be used after viewing a performance of an original play written and performed by visiting high school students.

Source: From *Developing Arts-Loving Readers* (p. 172) by N. L. McDonald and D. Fisher, 2002, Lanham, MD: Rowman & Littlefield Education. Used by permission.

Table 6.1 Lets Find Out About Strings (Vocabulary Chart)

Word	What I think it means	What it really means	Where I found out
strings			
bow			
tuning			
pegs			
fingerboard			
bridge			
sound hole			
plucked			
string family			
violin			
viola			
cello			
double bass			
fiddle			
string section			
orchestra			
rehearsal			
performance			

Note: This KWL chart was used with grades 4–8 as part of a unit about Children's Literature About String Instruments. The chart was used by students throughout their book-club activity and video viewing about strings and string musicians. As the students worked in small cooperative groups, they kept their individual knowledge charts handy. Some groups submitted their chart as a group effort; other groups decided to keep this assessment activity as an individual effort.

Source: From "Strings Attached: A Musical Listening Unit," by N. L. McDonald and D. Fisher, 2002, *Music Educators Journal, 88*(5), pp. 32–38. Reprinted with permission.

Progress Checks During Arts-Infused Activities

To avoid wasted time and off-task behavior, structure small-group or individual, graded progress checks (in the form of easily written checklists and descriptions). Progress checks allow you to see what has been accomplished so far in a project or activity and provide you with powerful indicators of how that learning is developing. These checklists can be used as a part of the overall student grade on the project (see Figure 6.2, "Multicultural Music Project—Progress Check #1 (middle school level).

FIGURE 6.2 Multicultural Music Project—Progress Check #1

Members of our group: _____, _____, _____,

_____, _____, _____, _____.

Culture: _____

Continent: _____

Hemisphere: _____

Language(s) Spoken: _____

Religion(s): _____

Approximate distance in miles from our city: _____

Please list who will be researching each area and the actual name of one book, website, CD or other resource that person intends to use:

Role of Music in this culture:

Names of native instruments (2–3 instruments)

Name of song or dance you will perform:

Name of story or legend you will read aloud or dramatize:

Name of food from this culture you will prepare and serve:

On the back of this page, create a paragraph which describes your report:

Source: From *Developing Arts-Loving Readers: Top 10 Questions teachers are asking about Integrated Arts Education* (p. 172) by N. L. McDonald and D. Fisher, 2002, Lanham, MD: Rowan & Littlefield Education. Used by permission.

Evaluative Discussion, Written Self-Assessments, and Journal Prompts

As part of their arts-infused activities, students are asked (in discussion, in rubrics and simple check lists, and through journal writing) to rate or consider/describe how things went and/or what they learned through their own or other's arts-infused activities. Within these reflective exercises, students also develop skills of critique, judgment, and valuing of their own and others' efforts and can thereby begin to formulate plans to improve their next efforts (See Figure 6.3, "Post-Performance Writing Prompts" (older students), and Figure 6.4, "Self-Assessment Inventory" (younger students).

Cross-Grade Performance Sharing/Exhibits

These are opportunities to share arts-infused activities, performances, displays, and projects. Students are able to expand their "audience base" and learn from others engaged in similar arts-infused processes. Evaluate in discussion and writing.

FIGURE 6.3 Post-Performance Writing Prompts: Attendance at a Play

After your students have attended or video-viewed a performance of a play by peers, high school, university, or community theatre groups, try using the following prompts for reflective writing tied to standards-based learning in the art of theatre:

• Describe the plot or story line of the play. What was the play about? What happened?
• Describe your favorite character. What did he/she do? How did he/she change during the play? What situations did he/she experience? Why did you like this character?
• Describe one favorite scene in the play. Name the characters involved, what happened, and how you felt about this action.
• Draw one of the play's scenery backdrops. Describe its importance to the play.
• Describe one of the following: favorite costumes, lighting effects, sound effects, surprise event, movement, or props. How did this add to the play?

Source: Adapted from *Developing Arts-Loving Readers* (p. 171) by N. L. McDonald & D. Fisher 2002, Lanham, MD: Rowman & Littlefield Education). Used by permission.

Displays of student artwork paired with original student writing. Displays of student art work and original writing can be developed through the use of select journal-writing prompts about those processes and "big idea" content learning. Invite other grades to visit your displays and performance sharing. Students can serve as "docents" and talk about their art and writing with other classes.

School-wide festivals/thematic arts activities. These are arts-based celebrations built upon various featured arts-infused, *topical curriculum content themes* (e.g., "The Night Sky," "Immigration/ Emigration to (Your City, Town, or State)," "Patterns in Nature and Math,") *or broader, more comprehensive conceptual themes* ("Tolerance," "Peace Makers," "Save Our Planet," "Our Natural World," etc.)

Student projects based on famous works of art. Projects based on the life and works of famous artists (musicians, dancers, actors) can include interesting facts and terms about that art and art-making processes and are displayed for class or schoolwide viewing.

6.1 Integrated Curriculum Themes and Concepts

For further reading and consideration of types of arts integration and thematic teaching, consult the following excellent sources:

Cornett, C. (2006). *Creating meaning through literature and the arts: An integration resource for classroom teachers* (2nd ed.). Upper Saddle River, NJ: Merrill/Prentice Hall.

Gelineau, P. (2004). *Integrating the arts across the elementary school curriculum.* Belmont, CA: Wadsworth.

Hancock, M. (2007). *A celebration of literature and response: Children, books, and teachers in K-8 classrooms.* Upper Saddle River, NJ: Prentice Hall.

Snyder, S. (2001). Connection, correlation, and integration. *Music Educators Journal, 87*(5), 32–39.

FIGURE 6.4 Self-Assessment Inventory

Name: _____ Date: _____ Grade: _____

Color the one most like you.

How am I doing at:

- looking up and using terms and concepts in art, music, drama, and dance?

  I am

  Super   Just OK   Needing Practice

- using vocabulary about the arts as I speak, write, and read?

  I am

  Super   Just OK   Needing Practice

- writing a summary of a video or live performance of art?

  I am

  Super   Just OK   Needing Practice

- taking notes while viewing performances of art?

  I am

  Super   Just OK   Needing Practice

- asking questions of teachers or friends to improve my comprehension?

  I am

  Super   Just OK   Needing Practice

- comparing and contrasting works of art?

  I am

  Super   Just OK   Needing Practice

- underlining new words as I read for recall?

  I am

  Super   Just OK   Needing Practice

- gaining comfort speaking, writing, and reading about the arts?

  I am

  Super   Just OK   Needing Practice

What type of help do I think I need?

Source: From *Developing Arts-Loving Readers: Top 10 Questions Teachers Are Asking About Integrated Arts Education* (p. 175) by N. L. McDonald and D. Fisher, 2002, Lanham, MD: Rowman & Littlefield Education.

In class word wall displays. Word wall displays are simple written lists or large vocabulary card displays of new vocabulary words. These lists are cumulative as the teacher "posts" new vocabulary as it occurs during a sequence of instruction and/or modeling. Word walls in this context may include arts-based vocabulary and definitions linked to "big idea" content and arts-infused project displays (hard copy, digital, computer/video based). These simple literacy-based displays incorporate student understanding of arts processes in connection to featured subject matter big ideas & vocabulary.

Community outreach or service projects. These are rich and varied opportunities for students to share what they learned in other subjects through an arts-based interpretation, display, performance, or demonstration.

● BEYOND THE CLASSROOM

School and Community Integrated Curriculum Displays

Agree with other teachers that the positive outcomes of any opportunity for students to share, display, view, learn from, and evaluate each other's work *far outweigh* any concerns you may have about "how well" your students drew or acted, sang, danced, etc.

For an on-line example of how one group of K–12 teacher peers displayed and described their thematic arts-infused lessons and curriculum units, visit *"The Art Exhibition at the SDSU Library: Arts through Literacy: People Who Have Made a Difference"* an online "virtual exhibit" made available through the San Diego State University Love Library Website: www.infodome.sdsu.edu/about/depts./spcollections/exhibits/0703/k12.shtml?print

Featured here are K–12 student's arts-infused activities in response to Children's and Adolescent Literature about people from the past and present who have made a significant difference in our lives, our community, country, and world.

Teacher Reflection

Teachers and future teachers can carefully reflect (in writing) on *how* and *what* the students learned within the arts-infused lesson and how that lesson and particular instructional techniques might be *improved*. They then use this written reflection within professional dialogues with methods class and school-site peers.

Summary of Examples of Assessment and Evaluation

By now, you have determined that assessment activities can and should be an integral part of the arts-infused lesson's overall meaning-making processes for both students and teachers. You have also noticed that *assessments can take many forms and can naturally occur before, during, and after arts-infused activities* through authentic assessments; written assessments; checklist surveys and discussion; tabulation through self and peer rating systems, rubrics, etc.

Assessments may also provide students and teachers rich opportunities for more evaluative, reflective thought, discussion, and written descriptions of the arts-process experiences, to determine and critique their affect toward increasing understanding of what students need to know.

Contributing Teachers' Assessments in Action

As previously mentioned, our contributing teachers participated in the same purposeful planning stages you have during the course of this book's self-study exercises. Let's return to two examples of how assessment/evaluation was woven into arts-infused lesson activities in their own classrooms.

• IN THE CLASSROOM

Integrating Social Studies/History and the Arts: "Jamestown in 1607"
Content Areas: History/Social Science, English Language Arts (Writing and Speaking), Arts (Theatre)

You may remember that Mrs. Crandall purposely sought to include standards-based, arts-infused, active learning opportunities constructed to include and result in authentic assessments (mini-performances of student work, created monologues about jobs and workers in Jamestown paired with class evaluation and self-reflection).

Mrs. Crandall developed a written exercise (i.e., graphic organizer) to become evidence of student understanding of content big ideas (social studies/language arts through theatre). (see Figure 6.5, "'Jamestown, 1607' Graphic Organizer: 'Trade Monologue Activity'". *In other words, Mrs. Crandall's assessments were naturally built into her purposeful plan for her lesson activities.* They were not separated from the students' actual arts-infused experiences and therefore became a natural, informative part of the actual lesson for both students and their teacher. This is assessment at its best.

How written and authentic assessments were used. In describing what actually happened during the "Jamestown, 1607" lesson, Mrs. Crandall provides the following activity sequence outline:

- Students read about trades in colonial times.
- Each student is *given* (no choices in Colonial times) a job to learn.
- Students research on computer for information on this trade and what the job entailed.

- Students fill out the graphic organizer (see Figure 6.5: " 'Jamestown, 1607' Graphic Organizer: 'Trade Monologue Activity' " (Colleen Crandall, Grade 5) to use as a format for their dramatization.
- Students synthesize research into the graphic organizer ideas they write.
- Students practice monologue for class presentations.
- Students perform presentations for classmates.

l e s s o n   t r a c k e r

Mrs. Crandall's "Jamestown, 1607"

Materials List (Text, Books, Website)
The following resources were used in Mrs. Crandall's grade 5 lesson:

History/Social Science Text

Macmillan/McGraw-Hill. (2007). *Social Studies* (National text series) *Grade 5: Our Nation*. New York: McGraw-Hill. (Unit 5: A New Nation)

Other Resources

Copeland, P. (1994). *Early American crafts and occupations coloring book*. Toronto, Ontario: Dover.

Fan, M., & Fan, B. (1997). *American made: The colonial child of 1740*. Annapolis, MD: Great American Coloring Book.

Kalman, B. (1992). *Historic communities: Colonial crafts*. New York: Crabtree. Website: www.crabtreebooks.com Phone: 1–800–387–7650

Kalman, B. (1998). *Colonial times from A-Z*. New York: Crabtree.

Notice the layers of process discovery within Mrs. Crandall's lesson and how *chosen assessments were purposefully built into many of the lesson stages*. For instance, when students were assigned a "job to learn," they had to access and incorporate what they already knew and what they just learned through their recent readings and Web searches. Because students were given a specific job topic, their focus was narrowed to an immediate, active, and possible learning goal—that is, to research and learn all they could about one person's job in 1607 Jamestown.

Through the natural and motivating end product of that research—a written assessment and accompanying individual oral presentation of "what they found out" in Figure 6.5, " 'Jamestown, 1607' Graphic Organizer: 'Trade Monologue Activity' "—students could make meaning of the facts they learned. Through that creative task, their work moved toward an interesting authentic assessment goal (individual trade monologues) involving active, dramatic, and expressive contexts for students to "show" what they found out and learned.

FIGURE 6.5 "Jamestown, 1607" Graphic Organizer: "Trade Monologue Activity" by Grade 5 Teacher, Colleen Crandall.

Name: _____ Date: _____ Room _____

Trade Monologue Activity:

Today, you will read about a trade people performed during colonial times around 400 years ago. You will look at any pictures and see if they can offer you insight about what the work this person did might have been like at that time. You can look up your occupation on the internet to learn more about your work. Finally, you will need to fill out this monologue and share it with the class. The words you write must give your audience a vision of what you do each and every day.

Differentiation: To further enhance your presentation, you may prepare PowerPoint slides with pictures from your research about your trade to show as you read your monologue.

The _____
(Name of your trade)

I am a _____ living almost 400 years ago during colonial times in the New World.

I make my living helping other people by _____.
(What do you do/make to help people?)

If you came to where I work you would see _____.
(What do you see people in the picture doing?)

Things I need to do my work include: _____.
(What tools are being used by the person in the picture to do this job?)

People in this area need my trade because _____.
(Why was this an important job in the community at that time?)

One thing people who are employed at my kind of work have to do every day is _____

_____.
(From the information you have, what do you infer this person would have to do every day?)

The thing I like most about my work as a _____ is _____
(Your trade)

_____.
(Write what you think might be great about your job.)

The hardest part of my work is _____
(Write what you think might have been really hard about the job you did every day.)

because _____.
(Write why you think this part of your job is so hard.)

I wish _____.
(Write what you wish you could be doing instead of this job—it has to be something a person could have done 400 years ago!)

If I could change something about the work I do, in the future, I would . . . _____

_____.
(How could you make this job easier? Is there something people know how to do these days that you could help teach this person to make their job easier?)

Your Job . . .

Now you will use the format of what you just wrote in the poem above and reenact the poem as a dramatization. You will act out as if you are actually this person doing the job you wrote about for the class. You will become this tradesperson and help the class experience "a day in the life of a _____."

Finally, and importantly, through these purposefully planned authentic assessments, students were able to view each other's work and learn "horizontally" with and from each other.

What happened? When asked what she observed during the processes of this lesson, Mrs. Crandall offered,

> My students researched the jobs colonists were engaged in and took their "characterization" task seriously. The students looked carefully at items in pictures from books and internet sites to discuss in their presentation what they [the Colonial worker] did and what tools they used in their daily lives to do their work. My students enjoyed being an expert about the trade information they had studied and shared with the class.

Mrs. Crandall lists the following ways she *assessed/evaluated student learning linked to the big ideas* her students needed to know:

> I used the graphic organizer and looked at the research the students printed out. I compared to see if materials/information they researched were included/synthesized into the graphic organizer. I then graded the presentation of that material in their performed monologue—oral presentation or dramatization.

In describing how she thought the use of the arts contributed to *student understanding* during this lesson, Mrs. Crandall adds,

> The acting out of the tradesperson was powerful because the audience who watched the performance got a better idea of what kind of work this person did and how hard the job was in terms of human energy.

Some of my students commented,

> "I can't believe how hard the people worked in those days!" (furniture maker)
>
> "That job was dangerous!" (blacksmith)
>
> "I couldn't eat food with maggots in it—yuck!" (crew member on a ship)

Another student wrote,

> "I liked going to the front of the class and telling everybody about my job as a blacksmith because we were studying about jobs during the colonial times. Everybody should know about all the jobs during the colonial times because it helped me understand how hard it was to do all these jobs. In my job, I made horseshoes, weapons, knives, tools for the farmer. I was important in the colony because if I wasn't there, they wouldn't have the tools they needed to do their work."

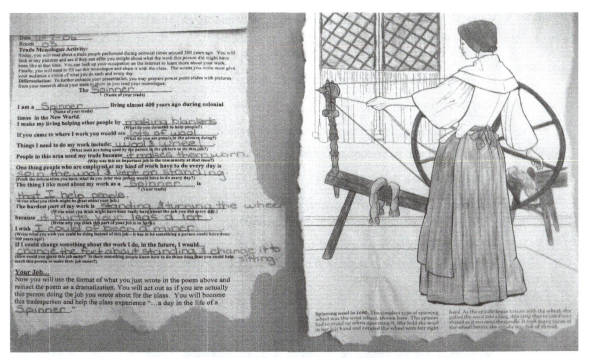

Sample of student work in Mrs. Crandall's "Trade Monologue Activity" lesson.

Photo by Colleen Crandall.

Finally, Mrs. Crandall shared her *personal reflection* about this lesson by saying,

> The project of having students perform as a tradesperson during colonial times was
> fantastic for them and their "audience" (the whole class). We all learned about things to
> do with tradespeople we didn't know before and it was fun seeing students take their
> role as the tradesperson and share what they did as this person during that time period.
> I loved the ownership they had of their tradesperson!

● IN THE CLASSROOM

Integrating Social Studies (Geography) and the Arts: "Desert Habitat Art" Grade 3 Content Areas: History/Social Science (Geography), Arts (Visual Art)

Remember that Mrs. Gray planned this "Desert Habitat Art" lesson within a series of
integrated lessons in a unit surrounding the instructional theme (social studies/geogra-
phy, life science, visual art) of "Where Living Things Are Found." In this lesson, Mrs. Gray
sought to infuse visual art activities (on-location sketching in a local desert garden and, later,

Contributing Teachers' Assessments in Action

watercolor media) into her social studies/science lesson because she "hopes [her] students will take their understanding to a deeper level."

Mrs. Gray's lesson's "big ideas" in Social Studies included the following:

● Students need to understand landforms (desert)

"Big ideas" in Science included:

● Students need to learn concepts of desert environments and habitats.

● Students need to understand ecosystems (desert).

Mrs. Gray wanted to use visual art activities to:

● Create (on-location/live) landscape sketches and watercolor paintings that will integrate students' understanding of habitats (desert).

● Help students learn new visual art media (watercolor) as they explore concepts of foreground, middle ground, and background and perspective as they create landscape paintings.

Mrs. Gray's third-grade student sketching outdoors before painting a "Desert Habitat" scene.
Photo by Kate Gray.

How written and authentic assessments were used. The assessment of this live, on-site arts-infused learning experience was purposely paired with a visual art-making process and product (desert sketches and watercolor). The assessment was designed to help students expressively communicate, make meaning, and remember what they learned about desert landforms, habitats, and environments. At the same time, students were given the opportunity to naturally experiment with, directly apply, and thereby increase their new knowledge and experience with visual art forms, processes, and media.

Finally, Mrs. Gray learned to look at these student processes and paintings to determine what and how students learned and how they expressed that learning through their artwork. Assessment, therefore, became a thread throughout the entire lesson—an informative, working vehicle for both students and teacher to communicate their understanding of the content big ideas.

What happened? In describing what happened, Mrs. Gray provides the following activity sequence outline:

- Students sketch desert plants at the community cactus garden while noticing landscape settings (mesas, canyons, mountains).
- Discuss foreground, middle ground, and background along with perspective.
- Students create (on watercolor paper) a horizon line using desert landforms in the background.
- Students lightly sketch onto watercolor paper desert plants and animals.
- Students discuss watercolor technique (mixing colors, adding colors).
- Students paint landscape.

l e s s o n   t r a c k e r

Mrs. Gray's "Desert Habitat Art"
Materials List
The following materials were used in Mrs. Gray's third-grade lesson:

History/Social Science Text
MacMillan/McGraw-Hill TimeLinks. (2000). *Communities.* New York: McGraw-Hill.

Trade Book
Guiberson, B. (1991). *Cactus hotel.* New York: Henry Holt.

When asked *what she observed during the processes of this lesson,* Mrs. Gray commented:

I narrowed the lesson so each student was creating a desert landscape. A benefit was the inclusion of the sketching component. I loved being able to take the students outdoors and explore beyond the classroom.

● BEYOND THE CLASSROOM

Arts in the Open Air

Make a list of places within your school grounds and in your community that may hold interesting visual environments for students to sketch, move, act, and make music (parks, museum grounds, public places, land features and vistas, etc.). If your space and availability to leave your school grounds is limited and/or restricted, why not create your own small outdoor refuge of some kind? Ask students what could be included (plants, rocks, bench) and work to create a simple, special place where (weather permitting) students could go to do independent work.

Mrs. Gray commented on *how she determined (assessed) student learning linked to the big ideas* her students needed to know:

Their actual paintings reflect the students' ability to integrate their understanding of landforms, habitats, and ecosystems. On the most basic level everyone painted a desert habitat. What was so interesting was how each piece was different. To me, this truly indicates that the students understood.

In describing *how she thought the use of the arts contributed to student understanding of big ideas during this lesson,* Mrs. Gray adds,

The students needed to integrate their understanding of land forms, habitats, and ecosystems in order to create something original. The medium allowed for students to express their understanding. Each piece was an individual assessment. Students were able to reflect on their learning and use it for themselves to create their own work of art.

After the lesson, *Mrs. Gray reflected on what she might do differently* by saying,

Relax! I'd never taught using watercolors and made assumptions about how it might go wrong. It can't go wrong. Each student did something different and each piece had something special.

Finally, Mrs. Gray shared her *personal reflection about the processes and final products* of this lesson by adding,

Their work was beautiful. Each student took their understanding and made something unique. They each had a vision of what they wanted to create. It was so powerful to see them take ownership of the work. I will do this lesson again next year.

Conclusion

True assessment can be a guide to our teaching—a touchstone, an informative measurement, and a reflective/evaluative indicator of what (and whether or not) our students have learned and understood. Purposefully planned assessments can also indicate *how* our students experience, make meaning of, apply, and remember content. Arts-infused activity naturally creates possibilities for assessment/evaluations of "what and how" our students experienced, created, and did as they directly applied their new knowledge within the expressive avenues the arts provide. And it is through these expressive avenues that your students will increase and deepen their understanding of content as they become more involved, active, and interested in the learning at hand.

Self-Study

Arts-Infused Lesson Assessments

Through the course of this chapter, you have explored many examples of active assessment (discussion, written, authentic) and have read about how two of our contributors planned and used forms of assessment during and after their arts-infused lessons. You also read their own (and their students) reflections about the arts-infused lesson activities and processes.

Now it's time for you to do the same! Although you began this assessment/evaluation process from the very beginning of your purposeful planning (and have already undoubtedly incorporated various forms of assessment during your actual lesson), the following form will provide you with further opportunities to think about, explore, write, and reflect on assessment/evaluation within this and other arts-infused lessons.

How to Use Figure 6.6, "Self-Study: What Happened? Assessments in Action"

In completing the Figure 6.6 Self-Study form at the end of this chapter, you might use the following sequence to guide your work: (continued to p. 150)

FIGURE 6.6 Self Study: "What Happened? Assessments in Action"

Name: _____

Methods Class or School Site: _____

Grade(s)/Subject: _____ _____

Title of Lesson Topic or Theme: _____

Content Area(s): Circle one or more: Social Studies   Science   Math   Language Arts/Literacy

DIRECTIONS: *This self-study is about the art-infused lesson(s) you have been purposefully planning throughout this book. Consult your Self-Study exercises from previous chapters as you answer the questions below.*

Which Art(s) were incorporated into the content area(s)?:

Circle one or more: Music   Dance/Movement   Visual Art   Drama/Theatre

Step-by-step through this lesson activity (what was actually done—sequentially):
(6–10 *very clear, short steps* as needed—write clearly, as though you were teaching a peer to replicate this lesson.)

Complete Materials List: (List *all* texts and trade books (title, author, date, publisher), CDs, videos, art supplies, etc., used within your lesson. Include websites and very short descriptions of what you found on each. The more accurate the info, the better.)

Assessment/Evaluation

What kinds of things did you observe during the processes of this lesson? How did it go? What worked? What didn't? (4–6 sentences)

How did you actually *assess/evaluate* student learning linked to the BIG IDEAS your students needed to know (and you identified) in this content area lesson? How do you know they learned and understood these big ideas? (Refer to your previous Self-Study forms from Chapters 1–5 of this book. List the big ideas for this lesson and then describe how you found out if the students learned them (or not). Remember that observation of process and final products of a lesson are a form of assessment.)

With hindsight, *what would you do differently* on this lesson? (2–3 sentences)

Reflections

In your personal opinion, *how* did your use of the art(s) contribute to student understanding in this lesson? WHY? (3–5 sentences)

Quotes from the students about this activity: (2–3 written or oral comments you collected)

Your personal thoughts about final products/process projects the students created—how will your classroom experiences with this lesson serve to shape your planning in the future? (Be specific: 3–6 sentences)

- Fill in the "Focus Activity" (anticipatory checklist) found at the beginning of this chapter. Compare your "After Reading Chapter" responses to your "before" responses.

- Discuss each question and your responses with a methods class or school-site peer. Be sure to express *why* you answered in the way that you did, and allow the other person to do the same (uninterrupted).

- Re-read, review, and have handy all the self-study materials you have filled in during exercises at the ends of Chapters 2 through 5. Refer to them as needed.

- Fill in the Figure 6.6, "Self-Study: What Happened?: Assessments in Action."

- Share your self-study responses with a methods class or school-site peer (via phone call, email, or in person). Really listen to others' responses.

- Keep (i.e., reconstruct) this self-study on computer or in hard copy to use within a personal file of arts-infused lessons you will begin to construct in the last two chapters of this book.

References

Bruner, J. (1966). *Toward a theory of instruction.* Cambridge, MA: Harvard University Press.

Bruner, J. (1973). *Beyond the information given: Studies in the psychology of knowing.* New York: W. W. Norton. (Original work published 1957)

Burz, H., & Marshall, K. (1999). *Performance-based curriculum for music and the visual arts: From knowing to showing.* Thousand Oaks, CA: Corwin Press.

Copeland, P. (1994). Early American crafts and occupations coloring book. Toronto, Ontario: Dover.

Cornett, C. (2006). *Creating meaning through literature and the arts: An integration resource for classroom teachers* (3rd ed.). Upper Saddle River, NJ: Prentice Hall.

Fan, M., & Fan, B. (1997). *American made: The colonial child of 1740.* Annapolis, MD: Great American Coloring Book.

Gelineau, P. (2004). *Integrating the arts across the elementary school curriculum.* Belmont CA: Wadsworth.

Guiberson, B. (1991). *Cactus hotel.* New York: Henry Holt.

Hancock, M. (2007). *A celebration of literature and response: Children, books, and teachers in K–8 class-rooms* (2nd ed.). Upper Saddle River, NJ: Prentice Hall.

Kalman, B. (1991). *Historic communities series: Colonial crafts.* New York: Crabtree.

Kalman, B. (1997). *Colonial times from A–Z.* New York: Crabtree.

Macmillan/McGraw-Hill. (2007). *Social Studies (National text series) Grade 5: Our Nation.* New York: McGraw-Hill.

McDonald, N., & Fisher, D. (2002). *Developing arts-loving readers: Top 10 questions teachers are asking about integrated arts education.* Lanham, MD: Rowman & Littlefield Education.

McDonald, N., & Fisher, D. (2006). *Teaching literacy through the arts.* New York: Guilford.

Ogle, D. (1986). K–W–L: A teaching model that develops active reading of expository text. *The Reading Teacher, 39,* 564–570.

Snyder, S. (2001). Connection, correlation, and integration. *Music Educators Journal, 87*(5), 3.

Wiggins, G., & McTighe, J. (2006). *Understanding by design* (2nd ed.). Alexandria, VA: Association for Supervision and Curriculum Development.

Unpacking the Arts Standards' Big Ideas

The arts are inseparable from the very meaning of the term "education." We know from long experience that *no one can claim to be truly educated who lacks basic knowledge and skills in the arts.*

—p. 5 of *Dance, Music, Theatre, Visual Arts: What Every Young American Should Know and Be Able to Do in the Arts: National Standards for Arts Education* (MENC, 1994).

FOCUS ACTIVITY

Directions: Please fill out before and after reading this chapter.

Before Reading Chapter A = agree D = disagree	Statements	After Reading Chapter A = agree D = disagree
	I am able to access and use state and/or district Arts content standards in Music, Dance, Theatre, and Visual Art.	
	Much of the language within the arts standards seems exclusively aimed at arts specialists and is not appropriate for classroom teacher use.	
	Arts content standards contain "big ideas" that can help me condense, group, understand, and teach/assess some of that content.	
	I know ways to plan, teach, and assess arts standards within arts-infused lessons across the curriculum.	

Built upon the foundations of your reading in this book and your own direct planning and teaching experiences with the arts, you are now able to take a more in-depth, comprehensive, and meaningful look at arts content standards. And by doing so, you may be able to establish clearer pathways toward understanding and using your own arts content standards within arts-infused lessons across the curriculum.

The Arts content standards will be "unpacked" and discussed and then directly applied within real-life contexts of arts-infused lessons in the K–8 classroom. As you read (and reflect later, in this chapter's Self-Study exercise), you will have opportunities to determine which of your *own* arts content standards are most appropriate and usable considering both your own "comfort zone" in the arts and what students need to know, do, learn, and remember.

Arts Standards in Purposeful Planning

Due to the breadth of discipline-specific content found within each of the four arts' standards (Music, Visual Arts, Theatre, and Dance), the following discussion is built on answering a number of questions below—those *most applicable* toward the purposeful planning purposes of this book.

What Are Content Standards in the Arts?

The original National Arts Standards are a statement of what K–12 students are to be able to do and know about all four arts disciplines (music, visual arts, theatre, and dance) and describe both content and achievement levels students should know and be able to do by the end of grades 4, 8, and 12. These standards have been adopted and/or adapted in forty-seven states and have been endorsed or supported by eighty national arts and arts education organizations: "The National Standards for Arts Education articulate goals for accomplishment long sought by teachers of the arts at all levels of education" (MENC, 1994, p. 1).

> **7.1 Note on Arts Standards**
>
> You will be given the opportunity to easily translate and make connections to your own arts content standards. As mentioned before, the *National Standards for Arts Education in Dance, Music, Theatre, Visual Arts: What Every Young American Should Know and Be Able to Do in the Arts* (MENC, 1994) will be discussed here. Those standards preceded and therefore shaped all state and district standards in the Arts. Since our contributing teachers teach in the state of California, some of that state's VAPA content standard language will also appear.

The arts standards articulate that *a true education in the arts includes education and experiences in the panorama of all four arts disciplines* (e.g., Gelineau, 2004; Jensen, 2005; MENC, 1994; Snyder, 2001). It is important to note that *an education in the arts* should not be confused with a visual arts education (one of the four arts). Instead, the word *arts* is a composite term encompassing *all four* of the arts disciplines. The writers of the National Standards in the Arts comment on the breadth of the content of each of the arts "recognizing that each of these encompass a wide variety of forms and sub-disciplines" (MENC, 1994, p. 1).

In 1990, "with the passage of the *Goals 2000: Educate America Act*, the national goals are written into law naming the arts as a core academic subject—as important to education as English, mathematics, history, civics and government, geography, science and foreign language" (MENC, 1994, p. 131). *Therefore, by law, a complete and comprehensive education in all four arts should be available for all our students.* Simply put, the arts are core content, therefore *all* students deserve and should have access to specialized instruction (an education in the arts) taught by specialists in all four arts disciplines.

For Whom Were Arts Standards Intended and What Is Their Purpose?

According to interview information obtained from Dr. Carolynn A. Lindeman (past president of Music Educators' National Conference and a member of the writing team for the National Arts Standards),

> The Arts Standards are designed to encourage achievement in each of the arts and provide benchmarks for how well students are learning and performing in the arts. They are to inspire excellence in teaching practices, goals, comprehensive planning, implementation, and assessment (e.g., Burz & Marshall, 1999; MENC, 1995, 1996). They give breadth to each of the disciplines and offer a comprehensive guide for teaching and learning. They also (through achievement standards within each content standard) clearly spell out levels of achievement students should reach throughout the grade levels. As such, they are rigorous in both design and content. (McDonald, 2008, p. 568)

However, as you know, if the delivery of a rigorously designed, specialized, and comprehensive content education (core curriculum) in all four arts for all our students is either threatened or has suffered complete elimination from the overall school curriculum, something else may be needed. It is increasingly obvious that classroom teachers have an important opportunity and role in teaching with and through the arts (arts infusion across the curriculum) so that more children will benefit from that learning over time.

What Do the Content Standards in the Arts Contain?

Each of the separate arts disciplines contain many subdisciplines and forms of that art and art-making processes.

In *music* these may include the following: singing, listening, playing of instruments, performance, composition, improvisation, analysis, aesthetic judgment, involvement in the music of many cultures and historical periods, songs in connection with other subjects, etc.

In the *visual arts* we can add sculpture, drawing, photography, painting, computer-based graphics, fabric design, ceramics, history, analysis and critique, connections to other arts and subjects, and much more.

Dance and *theatre* also contain performance, choreography, characterization, improvisation, critique and analysis, costuming, stagecraft, reader's theatre, script writing, and more (McDonald & Fisher, 2002, 2006).

Specific national content standards (without their various student-achievement-level standards listed) in each of the four arts (also known compositely as the instructional content area of "visual and performing arts") include the following:

National Music Content Standards include:

1. Singing, alone and with others, a varied repertoire of music
2. Performing on instruments, alone and with others, a varied repertoire of music.
3. Improvising melodies, variations, and accompaniments
4. Composing and arranging music within specified guidelines
5. Reading and notating music
6. Listening to, analyzing, and describing music
7. Evaluating music and music performances
8. Understanding relationships among music, the other arts, and disciplines outside the arts
9. Understanding music in relation to history and culture

National Dance Content Standards include:

1. Identifying and demonstrating movement elements and skills in performing dance
2. Understanding choreographic principles, processes, and structures
3. Understanding dance as a way to create and communicate meaning
4. Applying and demonstrating critical and creative thinking skills in dance
5. Demonstrating and understanding dance in various cultures and historical periods
6. Making connections between dance and healthful living
7. Making connections between dance and other disciplines

National Theatre Content Standards include:

1. Script writing by planning and recording improvisations based on personal experience and heritage, imagination, literature, and history
2. Acting by assuming roles and interacting in improvisations
3. Designing by visualizing and arranging environments for classroom dramatizations
4. Directing by planning classroom dramatizations
5. Researching by finding information to support classroom dramatizations

(continued)

Arts Standards in Purposeful Planning

6. Comparing and connecting art forms by describing theatre, dramatic media (such as film, television, and electronic media, and other forms)
7. Analyzing and explaining personal preferences and constructing meanings from classroom dramatizations and from theatre, film, television, and electronic media productions
8. Understanding context by recognizing the role of theatre, film, television, and electronic media in daily life

National Visual Arts Content Standards include:

1. Understanding and applying media, techniques, and processes
2. Using knowledge of structures and functions
3. Choosing and evaluating a range of subject matter, symbols, and ideas
4. Understanding the visual arts in relation to history and cultures
5. Reflecting on and assessing the characteristics and merits of their work and the work of others
6. Making connections between visual arts and other disciplines

Source: MENC, 1994, pp. 23–72.

As you read through these arts standards again (and then compare and contrast them to *your own* state or district arts standards), you have undoubtedly been reminded that *the defining premise of those standards' content and expectations are deeply rooted in distinct, specialized areas (disciplines) of study.* Within each area of the arts, the writers of the arts standards intended that *all* students have the opportunity to develop *competence* (doing and knowing) in each of the arts. *This, as you can imagine, requires specialized arts instruction by teachers who are specialists in the arts.*

But many of you may not have specialized training or expertise in one or more (or any) of these arts disciplines. The larger question, therefore, becomes, *"How can my purposefully planned arts-infused activities even begin to address the standards-based picture of what an overall education in each of the arts should contain?"* As you ponder this and other important questions, consider the following information.

7.2 Using Your State/District Arts Standards

Reference your state or district standards in the arts (VAPA—Visual and Performing Arts): Locate your arts standards online and keep them on-screen as you read the next section of this chapter. Compare the language, focus, and breadth of those standards to the discussion here (based on National Arts Standards and California VAPA Standards). Look for the "big ideas," not particular details.

Print out your online arts standards or use hard copy you already have in methods class or at your school site. *Checkmark those arts standards you understand the best, those that seem "doable" and appropriate for realistic use in your arts-infused lessons.*

The writers of the standards in the arts also, importantly, acknowledge, "A basic intent of the Standards is that the arts be taught for their intrinsic value. Beyond their significance in this arena, however, one of the most important goals the (Arts) Standards can achieve is to help students make connections between concepts and across subjects" (MENC, 1994, p. 13). Here you see the rationale for the important, potential role of standards-based, arts-infused learning opportunities within and across the K–8 general curriculum.

Can I Teach Arts Standards as a Nonspecialist?

It is important to acknowledge that arts activities connected in purposeful ways to other learning at hand (i.e., arts-infusion across the curriculum) *do not* take the place of what the arts standards define as a sequential education in the arts or disciplined-based learning in the arts. All students need and deserve a complete education in the arts. Rather than to be thought of as a poor substitution for discipline-based, comprehensive arts education, valid arts activity and instruction infused into the general curriculum may serve to provide *more* students *more* opportunities for increased involvement, engagement in, and synthesis, and memory of the learning at hand (Cornett, 2006; Hancock, 2007; Jacobs, 1989, 1997; McDonald & Fisher, 2002, 2006).

There is much you can teach about the arts as a nonspecialist. As you have read over and over again in the many lesson examples from our contributing K–8 classroom teachers, *much purposefully planned, standards-based learning about the arts does indeed take place within arts-infused lessons taught by nonspecialists like yourself.* You and this book's contributing teachers have accomplished much throughout this book's constructive self-study, teaching, evaluation, and reflection to ensure continued success in your efforts.

Furthermore, throughout this book's standards-based purposeful planning, you have laid the foundation for the worth and validity of these and future arts-infused learning opportunities within your own classroom.

Unpacking the Arts Standards

What Are Some Big Ideas Within the Arts Standards?

The question now becomes, "Which arts standards am I actually able to understand and teach in my arts-infused lessons?" In order to answer this question, some unpacking of those standards is needed. Viewed as "big ideas" (just as you have used standards-based "big ideas" from other content areas in all your purposeful planning), each of the arts includes standards that may be grouped into the following larger categories:

- Understanding, applying, and articulating the unique terminology, vocabulary, language, procedures, and technical aspects of that art and its art-making processes
- Creating, making, participating, and doing (i.e., performing) that art
- The ability to establish and make clear, purposeful connections to the various historical and cultural contexts of that art
- The ability to analyze, describe, articulate, critique, appreciate, and value the aesthetics of that art and the art-making processes and products involved
- The ability to establish and make clear, purposeful connections to other arts and content areas across the curriculum as well as lifelong learning and careers in the arts

The intent of this categorization is *not* to oversimplify arts content standards (as we know them to be both comprehensive and complex in breadth and depth), but rather to create manageable "big idea" groupings to enable you to successfully "unpack" the meaning of your own standards for your own classroom use. Viewed in this light, standards in the arts can be further streamlined into the following "big idea" categories:

"Big Ideas" Within Arts Content Standards

- **Understanding,** articulating, communicating, using and applying that art and art making processes
- **Creating**/doing/making that art
- **Connecting** that art to historical and cultural contexts
- **Valuing,** critique, assessing, describing, and making meaning of that art and art making processes
- **Connecting and establishing relationships** across the arts and other subject areas

---

Which "Big Ideas" in the Arts Standards Are Most Appropriate for *My* Personal Use and Why?

Remember that the "big ideas in arts standards" are meant to "unpack" or help group those standards' content into tangible concepts. As always, you will need to translate to your own standards.

Now refer to Table 7.1, "Unpacking the Arts Standards: Big Ideas" (pp. 160–162). In the left column of this table, you will see one of the arts standards' "big ideas." Next to that big idea you will see two examples of arts-infused activities related to this "big idea" from our contributing teachers' lessons. To the right of that, you'll find a short list of considerations (as a non-arts specialist) to use as you plan and teach within this "big idea" in the arts standards. These considerations are meant as "food for thought," as you will personally determine which standards' "big ideas" are most appropriate for your using the arts in your classroom.

> ### 7.3 What are the Big Ideas within my State/District Arts Standards?
>
> Do my own VAPA standards fit into these "big idea" groupings? You will most likely find that aforementioned "big idea" categories or groupings of the arts standards content can be readily applied to your own state and district standards. *Take a moment now to look over your own arts standards and compare them within the overall categories of the bulleted list in the text.* Do they fit? What does not fit? Discuss with a peer.

Discussion of Table 7.1: "Unpacking the Arts Standards' "Big Ideas"

Look at Table 7.1 again. Note that in the column to the right, "Considerations Affecting Your Planning and Teaching," suggestions have been thoughtfully offered based on feedback and data from many classroom teachers. You see that some of the considerations listed ask that you evaluate your own knowledge base and comfort zone in the arts and, if necessary, seek and locate resources to help with that particular "big idea" teaching and learning processes.

You were once again reminded that classroom teachers may need to possess an attitude of openness and experimentation as they teach with and through the arts. Simply put, according to our contributing teachers, considerable *courage and skill must be involved.* Courage and skill are needed to make and do arts with the students in your classroom, even though you may not feel secure, qualified, or experienced in doing so. Courage and skill are needed to learn to teach vocabulary, terminology, and various processes involved in making that art. Also, courage and skill are needed to connect learning with and through the arts to learning across your curriculum.

The good news is that, through the processes of this book's purposeful planning self-study and your own experimentation with arts-infused lesson(s) in your classroom, you already have exhibited the kind of courage, skill, and resourcefulness needed to explore the comprehensive territory of the Arts content standards. You have already thought about, planned, successfully used, and reflected upon the use of your own arts standards in your teaching.

Table 7.1 Unpacking the Arts Standards: Big Ideas

"Big Ideas" in All Four Arts	Applications of Arts Standards Within Contributing Teacher Lesson Examples	Considerations Affecting Your Planning and Teaching
Understanding, articulating, communicating, using and applying that art and art-making processes	1. **Visual Art:** Students *observe* an artwork. They learn and later apply new vocabulary about art terms (*line, shading, foreground,* and *background*) in their own sketches and later discuss and write about those processes. 2. **Dance:** Students learn and use (orally) vocabulary about dance (*force, energy, direction*) as they experiment with movement sequences for their original dances. Use dance in cross-curricular connection with math terminology and physical design and space.	• Teachers need to know, understand, and be able to demonstrate key vocabulary and art-making processes to teach and evaluate that learning. • This standard's "big idea" requires the teacher to have some direct experience and a "comfort zone" in making or doing that art (elements, processes, products, etc.) • Teacher "comfort zones" can be increased through collaboration with peers, inviting local guest artists to the classroom, attending workshops in the arts, consulting school/district arts specialists and resource teachers.
Creating, doing, making that art	1. **Music, Dance, Visual Art:** Students analyze song lyrics, illustrate song lyrics, learn to sing a memorized song, create original group dance sequence to that song, do performance sharing (music and dance) and displays of original art work about the song lyrics. 2. **Visual Art:** Students create an original work of art based on the observation of objects and scenes in daily life. They create (on-location/live) landscape sketches and watercolor paintings of desert habitats. They learn and apply new visual art media techniques (watercolor) as they explore concepts of foreground, middle ground, and background and perspective in their landscape paintings.	• Teachers need to be open-minded, nonjudgmental, and resourceful in developing their own and students' art-making skills. Experiment using *manageable* lesson expectations, content, strategies, processes, and evaluation (purposefully planned arts infusion). • Lesson content using this "big idea" should be matched to your own abilities and willingness to experiment within that art form's teaching and learning (art-making) processes. • Consult standards-based arts texts and materials and integrated arts instructional materials that are designed to clearly guide classroom teachers in hands-on arts activities. • After your own arts infused teaching, consult with peers and/or arts specialists or resource teachers for further ideas to enhance/improve your art-making processes and procedures.

| **Connecting** that art to historical and cultural contexts | 1. **Theatre:** Students participate in script writing and acting linked to characters within authentic historical periods and settings (Social Studies/History). Students learn characterization through writing and performing from a historical person's perspective and voice. Students interpret how theatre and storytelling forms (past and present) of various cultural groups may reflect their beliefs and traditions.

2. **Visual Art: Visual Literacy**—Students construct diagrams, maps, graphs, timelines, and illustrations to communicate ideas or tell a story about a historical event. They plan, create, and construct labeled maps with physical features of exploration routes. Students discuss and share artwork to aid group comprehension, identification, and application to other locations and exploration periods. | • Most classroom teachers are very good at establishing these connections. This "big idea" requires teachers and students to explore potential historical and cultural contexts in which the arts-infused activity may be grounded.
• Ask yourself, "What can I show or do to connect students to people, time, and places other than their own?"
• The arts and artifacts of other cultures and historical periods can serve as visual literacy tools connecting students in real and memorable ways to other times, people, and places.
• Search online and in social studies and other texts, video, and instructional workbooks to find authentic images (still and video, legends, stories, artworks, music, and dance), clothing, customs, language and poetry, and other historical/cultural elements linked to instructional themes and content at hand. |
| **Valuing,** critiquing, assessing, describing, and making meaning of that art and art-making processes | 1. **Music:** Students analyze song lyrics linked to other content at hand (e.g., math operations) for vocabulary and comprehension. Students sing and perform age-appropriate songs from memory. They create developmentally appropriate movements to express their knowledge of pitch, tempo, form, and dynamics in music. Students also create illustrations of song lyrics (poetry). After performance sharing, students engage in out-loud discussion (oral language) of artwork and music/dance processes.

2. **Visual Art:** Students discuss the various works of art that artists create and the type of media used (e.g., Eric Carle's colored paper collage.) They identify the elements of art (line, color, shape/form, texture, value, space) in the environment and in works of art, emphasizing line, color, and shape/form. Students create original artwork based on observations of actual objects. They use texture in two dimensional works of art. Afterward, students discuss works of art created in the classroom focusing on selected elements of visual art (e.g., shape/form, texture, line, color). They identify and describe various reasons for making art. | • Classroom teachers are very good at leading discussions, evaluations, and reflections about student art-making processes.
• Simply create opportunities for your students to share and evaluate (critique) their arts activity with others. Ask students to describe the processes they went through to create that art as they use terminology and concepts appropriate to that art-making task.
• Use reflection and evaluation activities (written, oral) you already use in other content area assessments. |

(continued)

| Connecting and establishing relationships across the arts and other subject areas. | 1. **Theatre:** Use theatrical skills to present content or concepts in other subjects (e.g., U.S. history/social science). Students write scripts of original plays based on authentic historical information about the topic (e.g., Westward Expansion).

Students act in, direct, and rehearse original plays in which they perform character-based improvisations, pantomimes, or monologues, using voice, blocking, and gesture to enhance meaning.

Performance and analysis of plays for and by peers.

2. **Visual Art:** Students learn and understand the lifecycle and parts of a butterfly and recognize external features of insects (Life Science).

Share information and ideas, describe butterflies (e.g., size, color, shape), locations, and actions (Language Arts/Oral Language Development).

Describe the roles of authors and illustrators and their contributions to print materials about insects (Visual Arts, Language Arts/Oral Language Development).

Students communicate observations orally and through drawings. Students create artwork based on observations of actual objects (insects = butterflies).

They discuss works of art created in the classroom.

Students identify and describe various reasons for making art (e.g., to express and interpret their observations of butterflies.) | • This "big idea" is easily applied by classroom teachers.
• *Because you have already planned an arts-infused lesson, you have already begun to establish natural connections and relationships between the arts and other content areas' standards-based "big ideas".* In other words, through your self-study exercises within this book, most of the groundwork has already been laid.
• Avoid *artificial* connections and relationships. Seek to connect learning across content areas by utilizing the arts to help students learn and remember the (standards-based) "big ideas" you know they need to know.
• Make *authentic* connections by calling to attention (through discussion, writing, etc.) what the arts activity taught students about the content learning at hand.
• Invite students to describe, write, and dialogue with peers about what they learned through the arts activity.
• Ask students to connect how and what they did, performed, or made in arts activities to the correct vocabulary, facts, terminology, and concepts in the content theme at hand (e.g., math, social studies, etc.).
• Encourage more learning connections as students use *appropriate art(s) terms and concepts involved.* |

Conclusion

This chapter began with a discussion of the arts standards (Music, Visual Art, Theatre, and Dance). You read about how the writers of these standards intended that every child in every school should receive a standards-based, sequential education in all four arts, taught by teachers trained and specialized in the content and teaching of those arts.

You also read about the reality that all students *may not* be receiving specialized instruction in all (or sometimes *any* of) the four arts. Therefore, something else may be needed to deliver *more* arts to *more* children.

Classroom teachers can teach with and through standards-based arts activities in order to establish important connections and relationships to learning across the curriculum. Our contributing teachers (and you) have provided evidence that nonspecialists can and do find success within purposefully planned lessons in which standards-based arts activity becomes an important avenue for learning across the curriculum.

Finally, in this chapter's self-study exercise, Figure 7.1, "Self-Study: Review of My Visual and Performing Arts Standards", you will have a rich opportunity to build upon your current knowledge and awareness of what your own (or future) grade-level arts standards contain. The length of this self-study is longer, yes, but by taking the time to complete these research and reflective activities, you will be able to establish which arts standards are most appropriate (and why) for use in your own and future classroom.

Self-Study: Review of My Visual and Performing Arts Standards

Suggestion for Using Figure 7.1

Consult your previous self-studies (hard copy or on computer). Your past work will guide you in completing Figure 7.1.

- As a starting point, revisit the "Focus Activity" at the beginning of this chapter. Answer in the right-hand column ("After Reading Chapter"). Discuss with methods class or school-site peer.
- Refer to your previous self-study exercises.
- Locate, online or in hard copy, the visual and performing arts standards for your district or state. Depending on your state or district, most content standards can be found online at district websites. (continued p. 168)

FIGURE 7.1   Self-Study: Review of My Visual and Performing Arts Standards

IMPORTANT NOTE: There are *multiple sections* of this self-study. It is best to complete all sections in the order you see here.

Name: _____

Methods Class or School Site: _____

Grade(s):_____

Title of Lesson/Topic, or Theme: _____

Directions: *The following questions refer to the arts-infused lesson(s) you have planned and taught throughout the course of reading this book and/or taught in your method's class teaching labs.*

Which of your district/state standards in the Arts were/are used in your own arts-infused lesson(s)?

Fill in the following table for one of your lessons:

NAME OF LESSON: _____

Name of Art Used (Circle the name of the art(s) you used below and fill in the columns to the right.)	EACH Art(s) Grade Level Standard Used (list #s and write out each standard)	Why this standard?
MUSIC		
VISUAL ART		

THEATRE		
DANCE		

NEXT: Review your grade-level arts standards in EACH of the Arts (Music, Visual Art, Theatre, Dance). **Print out a hard copy** of those standards. On that hard copy, **place a check next to the standards you feel most comfortable addressing. Place an "X" next to the standards you do NOT feel comfortable addressing.**

NEXT: Fill in the *entire* chart below (all four arts) to determine your personal **"Comfort Zone"** standards (those Arts standards you feel you can address ("doable") in your arts-infused teaching.

"Comfort Zone" Arts Standards

Name of Art Used	"Comfort Zone" Grade-Level Standards That Seem "Doable" (list #s and write out each standard)	Why?
MUSIC		

(continued)

VISUAL ART		
THEATRE		
DANCE		

NEXT: Fill in the chart on the following page to determine your personal "NON-Comfort Zone" regarding arts standards (those Arts standards you feel you **cannot or are unable to successfully address** in arts-infused lessons across the curriculum.)

NOTE that the right-hand column has an additional question (*How/where might you seek resources or help in this area?*). This is an important question to answer.

"NON-Comfort Zone" Arts Standards

Name of Art Used	"Non-Comfort Zone" Grade-Level Standard (list #s and write out each standard)	*Why* is this standard uncomfortable for you? *Where* might you seek resources or help in this area?
MUSIC		
VISUAL ART		
THEATRE		
DANCE		

If not, simply search your state's Department of Education and look for content standards in the arts or visual and performing Arts. Then locate your particular or preferred future grade level. You may need to do the same as you search in *each* of the four arts (Music, Visual Art, Theatre, and Dance). Have this information handy as you answer the questions on the self-study.)

● Now answer each of the questions in Figure 7.1, "Self-Study: Review of My Visual and Performing Arts Standards." *Be patient. This is a thorough review process and includes different sections.*

● Discuss your answers with methods class or school-site peers. Some of this discussion can be done on the phone or in short email exchanges. (What is important here is to continue the reflective work you have done with others throughout this book. By doing so, you will further expand your own knowledge about the arts standards.)

References

Burz, H., & Marshall, K. (1999). *Performance-based curriculum for music and the visual arts: From knowing to showing.* Thousand Oaks, CA: Corwin Press.

Cornett, C. (2006). *Creating meaning through literature and the Arts: An integration resource for classroom teachers* (3rd ed.). Upper Saddle River, NJ: Prentice Hall.

Hancock, M. (2007). *A celebration of literature and response: Children, books, and teachers in K–8 classrooms* (2nd ed.). Upper Saddle River, NJ: Prentice Hall.

Jacobs, H. H. (1989). *Interdisciplinary curriculum: Design and implementation.* Alexandria, VA: Association for Supervision and Curriculum Development.

Jacobs, H. H. (1997). *Mapping the big picture: Integrating curriculum and assessment K–12.* Alexandria, VA: Association for Supervision and Curriculum Development.

Jensen, E. (2005). *Arts with the brain in mind* (2nd ed.). Alexandria, VA: Association for Supervision and Curriculum Development.

Gelineau, P. (2004). *Integrating the arts across the elementary school curriculum.* Belmont CA: Wadsworth.

McDonald, N. (2008). Standards in the arts and arts within literacy instruction. In J. Flood, S. Brice-Heath, & D. Lapp (Eds.), *The handbook of research on teaching literacy through the communicative, performing, and visual arts, Volume II* (pp. 567–572). Mahwah, NJ: Lawrence Erlbaum.

McDonald, N., & Fisher, D. (2002). *Developing arts-loving readers: Top 10 questions teachers are asking about integrated arts education.* Lanham, MD: Rowman & Littlefield Education.

McDonald, N., & Fisher, D. (2006). *Teaching literacy through the arts.* New York: Guilford.

Music Educators National Conference (MENC). (1994). *Dance, music theatre, visual arts: What every young American should know and be able to do in the arts: National standards for arts education.* Reston, VA: Author.

MENC. (1995). *Strategies for teaching,* 13 vols. (C. Lindeman, [Ed]). Reston, VA: Author.

MENC. (1996). *Performance standards for music grades preK–12: Strategies and benchmarks for assessing progress toward the national standards.* Reston, VA: Author.

Snyder, S. (2001). Connection, correlation, and integration. *Music Educators Journal, 87*(5), 3.

Arts Within My Classroom and Beyond

You must be the change you want to see in the world.

—Mahatma Gandhi

FOCUS ACTIVITY

Directions: Please fill out before and after reading this chapter.

Before Reading Chapter A = agree D = disagree	Statements	After Reading Chapter A = agree D = disagree
	I plan to teach more arts-infused lessons in the future.	
	I would like to create and share a customized lesson file of arts-infused lesson ideas.	
	Others at my future or present school site may be interested in teaming efforts to offer arts-infused content teaching.	
	School-site administration, district leadership, and parents will be supportive of arts-infused lessons across the curriculum.	
	My surrounding community offers many resources for use in arts-infused teaching. I am able to locate and use those resources.	

This last chapter will guide you to create and use a customized lesson file of arts-infused lessons across your future or current K–8 classroom curriculum. Suggestions will be made for how to share this file with peers in your methods class and at school sites.

Next, ideas for increasing opportunities for arts infused teaching and learning in individual classrooms and beyond will be offered. This last chapter will conclude through the voices of our K–8 contributing teachers within a series of inspiring "thumbnail sketches"—brief outlines of additional lessons these teachers have purposefully planned, taught, and evaluated in their own classrooms.

Creating, Using, and Sharing Your Customized Lesson File

Through the processes you have completed throughout this book's Self-Study exercises, you are now ready to organize and document your arts-infused lesson(s) within a customized lesson file. *The purpose of constructing this customized lesson file is twofold:*

1. The file will help you to organize, plan, document, and evaluate teaching and learning within your customized arts-infused lessons.
2. Equally important, your file can easily be shared with peers (and vice versa) in your methods class and at your school site.

Please review Figure 8.1, "Suggestions for Creating and Using a Lesson File" (p. 172), a list of suggested steps to consider as you construct and eventually share your lesson file using Figure 8.2, "Arts-Infused Lesson File Form."

Now that you have considered the ideas in Figure 8.1, "Suggestions for Creating and Using a Lesson File", take the time now to fill in Figure 8.2, "Arts-Infused Lesson File Forms" (p. 174). Note that the latter portion of this form ("Peer Comment Sheet") should be filled out *after you have taught* a *peer's lesson* in either your methods class lab or at your school site.

Advocacy for Arts-Infused Teaching and Learning

The goal now is to expand on the original purposes of this book to include many other teaching peers. Those purposes are *to teach K–8 standards-based classroom content and meet student needs through the inclusion of arts activities as a powerful way to teach, learn, do, know, and remember.* Linked to this important purpose is to *increase both your and your students' understanding and knowledge of the arts themselves.*

According to our contributing teachers, as well as data collected from many K–8 classroom teachers across the country (McDonald & Fisher, 2002, 2006), in order for these purposes to happen, we should consider the following needs and actions:

Increase respect for the worth and value of arts infusion in K–8 general curriculum. Use information found in Chapter 1 of this book (and the many compelling, real-life examples of our K–8 contributing teachers) to create a grassroots statement of *why the arts are important in working toward increased student participation, involvement, and memory of the standards-based content learning at hand.* Use quotes from this book.

Inform current or future school-site leaders about the need for arts infusion within your curriculum. You and a few peers might schedule an appointment with a school-site administrator(s) to discuss why and how you would like to continue to teach with and through the arts. Invite site administrators to your own classroom to see student projects in action and view end products and performances/displays.

FIGURE 8.1   Suggestions for Creating and Using a Lesson File

1. Make multiple (many) photocopies of Figure 8.2, "Arts-Infused Lesson File Forms," or scan and store in your computer files.

2. Use your own lesson example(s) and self-study information from Chapters 2–7 of this book as you complete a sample "Arts-Infused Lesson File." You will notice this form's content abbreviates and condenses the components of purposeful planning covered within this book.

3. Make hard copies of your completed "Arts-Infused Lesson File" (Figure 8.2). Discuss and compare your work with a methods class or school-site peer. You may also share and compare form content online.

4. In your methods class labs or in your own classroom, actually teach a lesson a *peer* has created for his or her lesson file (and vice versa).

5. Then, both you and a peer can fill in a "Peer Comment Sheet" on each other's lesson and discuss. The "Peer Comment Sheet" is the third page of Figure 8.2, "Arts-Infused Lesson File Form." (Multiple copies of the "Peer Comment Sheet" should be placed in the lesson file, behind each lesson form, so that a running commentary can provide important feedback about each lesson.)

6. Create an email listserv of methods class or school-site peers to share lesson forms and peer comments online. Store all lesson file forms (with "Peer Comment Sheet") in your own computer files (i.e., "Arts-Infused Lessons") at home or at your school site.

7. Create and use a large portable lesson file or storage box system for your methods class or grade level/specialization at your elementary or middle school site. In those storage files, decide on a customized filing system to include "Arts-Infused Lesson File Forms." For example, our contributing teachers have filed lessons by grade-level content areas (math, science, etc.) further organized by standards-based, grade-level curriculum themes within content areas (e.g., "Westward Expansion," "Solar System," "Artist Study," "Patterns in Math").

8. Be sure that the contributors to this hard-copy file box or portable file include information or samples of appropriate materials to help other future teachers and/or practicing teachers actually teach that lesson. Be sure to include website addresses, where all books and resources are located, names and contact info on visiting guest artists, digital photos of actual processes of the arts-infused lesson, student worksheets, sample student art projects, etc.

Be sure to include student work and reflections in establishing your powerful case for the advantages of teaching with the arts.

Inform and involve parents in the effort.   Something as simple as a short Open House presentation in your classroom featuring examples of student work on bulletin boards, via PowerPoint presentation, etc., can serve to positively educate par-

9. Use the "Peer Comment Sheet" (in Figure 8.2) in the lesson file to add how you taught and evaluated another's lesson and provide any additional ideas and resources you and others personally incorporated into that activity. These are important opportunities for improving and augmenting individual arts-infused lessons. As such, the information on the "Peer Comment Sheets" are an important running record of how that particular lesson will evolve over time.

10. Store the file box of arts-infused lesson ideas in an agreed-upon methods class or school-site location where peers can easily "check out" materials from the file box. Be sure to also exchange lesson files via email.

11. Agree with methods class or school-site peers to set aside time to share arts-infused lesson activities from this file. One idea is to regularly share and model ideas at grade-level meetings at school sites. Curriculum sharing of this kind does not need to take a lot of time, but it may serve to inspire others to try some new arts-infused lesson ideas. This is particularly true if all lesson sequences and materials are made easily available.

12. Be sure someone brings the portable file or box to methods class or to school-site, grade-level meetings, etc., so that peers can see where lesson activities and materials are and how to contribute to "the cause." Do the same for online files. Actually show peers how to access and use the lesson files and how to add and use online resources related to particular lessons (e.g., websites, etc.).

13. In methods class or at school-site, grade-level meetings, one or more future or practicing teachers could share their arts-infused lesson forms as they talk through and show examples of student work and "what happened" in their lesson(s). Future and practicing teachers can create a PowerPoint of digital photos and/or video of students engaged in arts-infused lessons' activities and various end products of the lesson (artwork display, scans of student written responses, snippets of student acting and oral presentations, dancing, music making, etc.)

14. Agree to continue to share, model, and exchange arts-infused lesson ideas with peers on a regular basis (online, at future grade-level and staff meetings, visitations/exchanges in peers' classrooms, and informally in one-on-one discussion with peers.)

ents about how the arts can be successfully infused as powerful learning avenues in your classroom. Be sure to let parents know what you are doing in your classroom curriculum and what happens when students are fully engaged in learning with and through the arts. Be sure to also inform and solicit parents about contributing to your arts-infusion efforts (e.g., parent/grandparent guest artists [all four arts] in your classroom, art supplies from home, connections to community resources, etc.).

FIGURE 8.2 Arts-Infused Lesson File Forms

Arts-Infused Lesson File

Date: _____ Name: _____ Email address: _____

Methods Class or School site: _____

Grade or Subject: _____

Topic or Lesson Theme: _____

Name of this lesson: _____

Content Area(s) involved: _____

Content Area(s)' Grade-Level Standards addressed: _____

Art or Arts involved: _____

Grade-Level Art(s) Content Standards addressed: _____

What are some of the *big ideas* students need to know within content area theme this (other than the arts)? (Abbreviated list of 3 to 5 "big ideas")

Briefly state *how arts activities are infused* into this lesson:

List ALL materials used (including websites, book titles, authors, publishers, dates, CD titles, art supplies, people, resources, etc.).

Briefly and clearly list *teaching steps* in order of actual instruction:

How did you *evaluate/assess student learning* linked to the standards-based "big ideas" your students needed to know? How do you know they understood these big ideas?

In your personal opinion, how did your use of the art(s) activity contribute to student understanding in this lesson? WHY?

In hindsight, what would you do *differently* during this arts-infused lesson? Why? Be specific.

Peer Comment Sheet

DIRECTIONS: *After teaching a peer's arts-infused lesson idea, please fill in the following. Then add/attach/return to the lesson file box or online "Arts-Infused Lesson File" for this lesson by placing it right behind this other person's original lesson form.*

Lesson I used (name of lesson): _____

Name of person who wrote/created this arts-infused lesson: _____

Date lesson was taught: _____

My Name: _____

My Email Address: _____

Methods Class or School Site: _____

Grade Level or Subject Taught: _____

How did this lesson's arts activities increase student understanding of content involved?:

Suggestions to improve this lesson (planning, teaching and assessment):

List materials I've added to this lesson idea: (Attach hard copy or computer files of any resources you added to or used in this lesson.)

Develop a simple model-lesson presentation for other teachers or future teachers, interested parents, and administrators at your school site.   Lead a hands-on, arts-infused lesson at a professional growth day or other event at your current or future school site. Allow other future or classroom teachers to see you and a few peers actively teaching the type of standards-based lessons you have constructed during your work in this book. *Be sure the lesson results in some kind of end product and that you provide adult participants the opportunity to debrief the experience in a simple way.* Ask important questions during the "debriefing" (e.g., *What happened? How the did the arts activity increase our participation, involvement, and memory of the learning at hand?*)

Ask school-site administrators, district supervisors, and curriculum coordinators for a list of all arts resources and materials available for classroom teacher use.   Be sure to start your materials and resource search with a list of what you already have at your future or current school site. Talk to arts specialists teachers at school sites. Find out where district arts supplies, materials, and texts are located. Learn which local artists and performers may be contracted by your district and other school sites for artist-in-residence instruction, arts education, educational performances, etc.

Ask for time for professional growth and curriculum development in the area of arts infusion across the curriculum.   You and others might ask for a regular time slot (5–10 minutes or so) at grade-level or staff meetings when you can informally share how the arts are used in your classroom. As mentioned earlier, bring the arts-infused lesson file box and information to the meeting so that peers may be reminded that materials are there for them to use.

Ask for professional growth days or district teacher training in Arts Integration or arts infusion across the K–8 curriculum.   *Find out if your current or future district's arts coordinator or resource teacher will lead future and/or practicing classroom teachers in integrated lessons across the K–8 curriculum.* (Check with your university professor, and invite district arts resource specialists to come to your university methods class.) Also contact your local community college or university to locate teacher educators who are able to work with future and practicing classroom teachers to develop arts-infused curriculum.

Ask other grade-level peers if they would like to explore the idea of teaming/rotating arts-infused lessons across their curriculum.   For instance, some of our contributing teachers have participated in grade-level team efforts in which students in four classes are rotated through four teachers' lessons, each using one of the arts (music, visual art, dance, theatre). So, students have the benefit of exploring the same classroom content in a variety of artful ways. Participating "integration" team teachers enjoy the advantage of preparing one arts-infused lesson that is repeated four times (to include all four classes) over a span of one or more weeks.

Form an integrated arts committee at your school site. Our K–8 contributing teachers were volunteer members of a larger integrated arts curriculum committee for a total of five years. During that time (three times per year), teachers were released from their classrooms to attend professional growth seminars lead by the author of this book. During those meetings, arts projects were developed, arts-infused lessons and units were peer modeled and shared, grade-level standards-based curriculum was developed, and needs assessments and future planning were designed.

Our contributing classroom teachers cite this committee collaboration as an important positive influence on their ability to continue to include the arts within their classroom curriculum. For an example of their work together, see the online version of a K–12 thematic curriculum display at their local university's main library—"The Art Exhibition at the SDSU Library: Arts Through Literacy: People Who Have Made a Difference"—a PowerPoint slide presentation printout of the online "virtual exhibit," made available through the San Diego State University Love Library website: www.infodome.sdsu.edu/about/depts./spcollections/exhibits/0703/k12.shtml?print

"Thumbnail Sketches": Additional Ideas From Our K–8 Contributing Classroom Teachers

Curriculum reform of any kind begins with a personal professional commitment to change. Our contributing teachers' generous contributions to this book have been profound, to say the least. Through reading the constructive stages of their lessons, you have undoubtedly been well connected to the real-life needs of your future or current students.

What follows now are "thumbnail sketches" of more lessons by the same contributing teachers. These additional lessons will appear within *highly abbreviated structures* (templates) so that you can easily and quickly scan and grasp the main idea and intent of each arts-infused lesson. There, you will read what was intended, what happened, and the effects of that standards-based arts-infused learning on student understanding.

Make any needed translations to your own grade-level standards, student needs, and instruction. Also consider that the "thumbnail sketches" about arts-infused lessons in *other* grades and *subject matter* (other than your own) may indeed serve as a catalyst for your own future planning considerations.

THUMBNAIL SKETCH 1: **Ms. Tanonis**

Teacher: Ms. Rose Tanonis   **Grade Level/Subject:** Grade 1

Name of the Arts-Infused Lesson: "Patterns"

Content Areas Involved: Math (repeating patterns)

Arts Used: Music and Movement

Materials Used: Any "days of the week" or months of the year type song, teacher-made assessment to match number patterns with days and months, 9" × 12" laminated construction paper with the days of the week, months of the year, and numbers 1–12 printed on them.

"Big Ideas": By the end of this arts-infused lesson, my students will know and be able to do the following: Sing, move, read, and understand the word patterns for days of the week and months of the year.

Lesson Steps: Sing and teach the songs to your students. For morning opening, we sang the "Days of the Week" and "Months of the Year" songs every day. We used our fingers for the seven days of the week and put one up at a time as we sang Sunday, Monday, Tuesday, Wednesday, etc. We did the same for the months of the year, but once we sang October (month #10), we pointed to each of our cheeks for dimples to represent November (month #11) and then December (month #12)! Later, I made word cards and handed them out before singing. As we sang, the children would come up with the correct word or number. One student would have the number that represented the day or month; the other would have the word.

What Happened? How did the arts-infused activity add to students' understanding? I watched and listened as each child took the individual assessment and sang and matched the numbers to the correct day or month. The students know what each day and month word meant. They could read them with ease. They had seen them and used them so much with the opening songs and in their daily journals that the words were now automatic. My students are English language learners and learn best through as many modes as possible. This lesson is oral, auditory, visual, tactile, and kinesthetic. I am applying this technique more and more with songs and patterns. I am trying to make learning more fun and to implement things that really work for my kids.

THUMBNAIL SKETCH 2: **Mrs. Laws**

Teacher: Mrs. Adrienne Laws   **Grade Level/Subject:** Grade 2

Name of Arts-Infused Lesson: "Animal Adaptations"

Content Areas Involved: Science

Arts Used: Theatre, Music, and Movement (Dance)

Materials Used: Websites: www.yahooligans.com (research),
http://swbg-animals.com/fun-zone/index.htm# (Sea World Songs),
www.sandiegozoo.org/kids/index.html (adaptation games, crafts, activities),
www.harcourtschool.com/index.html (science activities)

**"Big Ideas": By the end of this arts-infused lesson, my students will know
and be able to do the following:** Through cadence chants, poetry, movement, and songs, students will know and remember at least three animals
from each group (mammals, reptile, amphibians—warm-blooded vs. cold
blooded) and explain at least two adaptations that help this animal survive in
its environment.

Lesson Steps: We made a KWL chart about mammals, reptiles, and amphibians. The chart, along with the grade 2 standards, drove my instruction. I down-
loaded cadence chants, songs, and poetry from the Sea World website. I made
these into posters and we learned one a day. Some we made movements to,
others we clapped out or snapped out. I met with an educator from the zoo, and
she gave me a copy of the cadence chants they use in their educational program
(e.g., "I'm a snake so long and thin, I have scales and shed my skin!") We sang
these like they do in military boot camp style. We used posters and made up
movements just like we did with the Sea World chants. The posters with these
words were hung around the room so students could revisit the information
during Read Around the Room Time or Free Choice Reads. Students paired up
and researched one animal from each group. They used website information.
Their assignment was to present to the class their animals: why the animal was
a reptile, mammal, or amphibian (i.e., characteristics—warm-blooded, etc.) and
at least two adaptations.

**What Happened? How did the arts-infused activity add to students' under-
standing?** Partnering students up allowed for a greater experience of success
in the written portion as well as the oral component. The students were introduced to challenging content vocabulary and were able to remember it because
it was embedded in a rhyming chant.

THUMBNAIL SKETCH 3: Mrs. Gray

Teacher: Mrs. Kate Gray   **Grade Level/Subject:** Grade 3

Name of Arts-Infused Lesson: "Where Living Things are Found"

Content Areas Involved: Language Arts/Literacy, Science

Arts Used: Dance and Theatre

Materials Used: *The Seed and the Giant Saguaro* by Jennifer Ward (2003, Rising Moon) and *The House That Jack Built* by Diana Mayo (2001, Barefoot Books)

"Big Ideas": By the end of this arts-infused lesson, my students will know and be able to do the following: Recreate the story of *The Seed and the Giant Saguaro* using props and movement. Recognize elements of a cumulative tale. Know examples of diverse life forms that live in the desert.

Lesson Steps: Introduce the elements of cumulative tales such as *The House that Jack Built*. Read aloud the story *The Seed and the Giant Saguaro* by Jennifer Ward. I created a reader's theatre script of the story that we then read as shared reading. My students practiced reading the script with fluency and expression. We created paper masks and/or props for each "speaker" in the book's reader's theatre. We performed the reader's theatre for other classes and asked for their feedback.

What Happened? How did the arts-infused activity add to students' understanding? My students became very familiar with the format of a cumulative tale. They were able to identify other cumulative tales and patterns based on their experiences in this lesson. They also know different plants and animals that live in a desert ecosystem. My students had the opportunity to practice fluency and expression. Students who normally don't like to share with the whole group were able to participate in a comfortable and predictable way. I liked that other classes gave my students feedback about their reader's theatre performance. Sometimes teachers are broken records. The comments were more valid coming from their peers. We will draw from this experience next time we perform for a group. Though the lesson changed over time, I liked the final results. The students were able to have fun and practice their skills.

THUMBNAIL SKETCH 4: **Mr. Pham**

Teacher: Mr. Khanh Pham   **Grade Level/Subject:** Grade 4/5

Name of Arts-Infused Lesson: "Folktales/Tall Tales"

Content Areas Involved: Language Arts, Social Studies

Arts Used: Visual Art

Materials Used: *American Tall Tales* by Adrien Stoutenberg (1976, Puffin) (book for shared reading—1 copy per student or 1 copy for the teacher for a Read Aloud); blank U.S. map found at www.eduplace.com/ss/maps/pdf/us_nl.pdf; physical map of the U.S. in *California: Adventures in Time and Place* (2000, McGraw-Hill); VHS tape of *Pecos Bill*, © 1988 Rabbit Ears Productions, Inc.; CD recording of the song "This Land Is Your Land" by Woody Guthrie.

"Big Ideas": **By the end of this arts-infused lesson, my students will know and be able to do the following:** Demonstrate map skills, separate fact and fiction, identify physical features and landforms. Students will list and illustrate major landforms mentioned in a story.

Lesson Steps: Review concept/definition of fact and fiction. Do a Shared Reading of "Sky-Bright Axe/Paul Bunyon" from *American Tall Tales*. Create a list of major landforms in the United States as they are mentioned in this story. Discuss the landforms and locate them on a U.S. map. Give each student a copy (blank) of the U.S. map to fill/draw in the landforms in the proper location. Fill in additional landforms as additional stories are read. Show a video of the corresponding tall tale following each story (e.g., "Pecos Bill"). Listen to and sing the song "This Land Is Your Land."

What Happened? How did the arts-infused activity add to student's understanding? My students were better able to visualize the physical features of America. In addition, my students gained better map skills. Students were not only able to show and locate these physical features, but also see in which state these physical features are located. I now incorporate a weekly patriotic song into my morning routine. Songs like "This Land Is Your Land" help bring into light these physical features of America.

THUMBNAIL SKETCH 5: **Mrs. Crandall**

Teacher: Mrs. Colleen Crandall   **Grade Level/Subject:** Grade 5

Name of Arts-Infused Lesson: "Colonial Social Life"

Content Areas Involved: Social Studies, Language Arts

Arts Used: Visual Art and Theatre

Materials Used: Search the following Colonial Williamsburg website to locate "A Day in the Life Series" for teacher resources: http://www.history .org/ History/teaching/dayinthelife/DayintheLife.cfm Look for historical paintings, video re-enactments and writings about life in American Colonial times in your school library and district resource center.

"Big Ideas": By the end of this arts-infused lesson, my students will know and be able to do the following: Observe and interpret colonial social life from observing a piece of visual art (historic paintings) from that time period. Be able to discuss the artists' perspectives. "Become" the characters in the historic art-works by creating and presenting a dramatic tableau to their classmates.

Lesson Steps: Teach concepts of colonial economy. Use overhead transparency/docucam/pictures from the Internet to show historic paintings from the colonial time period. Students write on paper what they observe is going on in each painting ("What is the artist's point of view from what you observe?"). After writing about all of the paintings, each group of five to six students stands and "becomes" a character in tableau representation of a selected historic painting. Each character then talks to the audience (classmates) about who he or she is and what he or she are doing in the scene of that historic painting.

What Happened? How did the arts-infused activity add to students' understanding? The art gave the students a character from that time period to "become" and take on the ideas and thoughts of a person. My students were able to synthesize things they had learned as they interjected those ideas into the character they played in their tableau. I was thrilled the students got into the parts of the characters as well as they did since they had never done this before. In the future, I would like to have students do a tableau around the writing of the Constitution and have them be the representatives from different colonies and their wives too. What would it have been like for these women?

THUMBNAIL SKETCH 6: **Ms. Elemont**

Teacher: Christi Elemont   **Grade Level/Subject:** Grade 6 Math

Name of Arts-Infused Lesson: "Probability Mosaic Art Piece"

Content Areas Involved: Math, Language Arts/Literacy

Arts Used: Visual Art

Materials Used: M&M candies; *Probably Pistachio* by Stuart J. Murphy (2001, HarperCollins); *McGraw-Hill Mathematics* by Gunnar Carlsson and Ralph L. Lohen (2002, Macmillan/McGraw-Hill); www.forbeyart.com

"Big Ideas": By the end of this arts-infused lesson, my students will know and be able to do the following: Express probability in four ways: as a ratio, fraction, decimal, and percentage and be able to convert back and forth. Express that events can be certain, likely, or unlikely. Students will learn how to make and justify predictions. Learn about and analyze these math concepts by creating and analyzing their M&M, colored-mosaic art pieces.

Lesson Steps: Start the class with a warm-up on probability where students use words such as "certain, likely, unlikely, and possible" to get them thinking. Read the book *Probably Pistachio* as a Read-Aloud to the whole class. (Practice beforehand and put Post-its in the book at points you want to stop and discuss important events.) Introduce mosaic art pieces via a PowerPoint slide show. Review conversions of fractions to decimals to percentages before passing out written work. Pass out probability worksheets to each student and have them predict the number of M&M's they will receive and how many of each color. Pass out one pre-made bag to each group and have them record their probabilities. Then, have them express it as in ratio, fraction, decimal, and percentage formats. When their worksheet is finished, have the team create two mosaic pieces. Take pictures to create a class probability-mosaic art book!

What Happened? How did the arts-infused activity add to students' understanding? It helped spark an interest in probability with the students. They were amazed how mosaic art connected with probability. Also, connecting literature to the beginning of a lesson can really win student buy-in and trigger prior knowledge because of the many situations that were introduced in the book. When the students were creating the art pieces, they had their math sheet next to them to remember the content it connected to. I absolutely loved teaching this lesson! The final pieces were outstanding and the students really appreciated mosaic art. This lesson and the kids' reaction to it really opened my eyes to including art connections in my future lessons.

THUMBNAIL SKETCH 7: **Mr. Soto**

Teacher: Mr. Andy Soto   **Grade Level/Subject:** Grade 8 U.S. History

Name of Arts-Infused Lesson: "Bill of Rights"

Content Areas Involved: U.S. History

Arts Used: Visual Arts and Theatre

Materials Used: Long strips of white construction paper, colored pencils and marker pens; *History Alive!: The United States* by Diane Hart (2002, Teacher's Curriculum Institute) and *The American Journey* by Appleby, Binkley, Broussard, McPherson, and Ritchie (2006, McGraw-Hill/Glencoe); www.unitedstreaming. com (a variety of video clips of the Bill of Rights and the U.S. Constitution)

"Big Ideas": By the end of this arts-infused lesson, my students will know and be able to do the following: Understand their basic liberties and rights established by the U.S. Constitution (Bill of Rights). Understand the amendment process of the U.S. Constitution. Create comic strips to show what they have learned about the Bill of Rights.

Lesson Steps: Prior knowledge/connection: Students discussed questions in small groups—What rights do you have at home, in school, and in your community? Then, a class discussion of the same. Brief overview/summary of content and present vocabulary terms (8–10 minute PowerPoint presentation). Reading/shared reading and note taking on graphic organizers. Comic strip activity and then comic strip presentations (students actually acted out their comic strip) for the whole class.

What Happened? How did the arts-infused activity add to students' understanding? The arts activities of making a comic strip and theatre presentations of the same are what sold this lesson! My students were hooked from the very beginning when I told them they would be creating and performing a comic strip. I guess the arts component was the engaging KEY for them wanting to learn. I will definitely use this lesson again. Most of my students did an excellent job. Even my low readers and English learners demonstrated comprehension of the standards, big ideas, and objectives of the lesson. Comic strips and performances of the comic strips can be used in almost any lesson.

Conclusion

In this final chapter, you have been provided a framework for creating a customized arts-infused lesson file. You also considered many suggestions for how to share lesson ideas among peers and how to broaden the base of advocacy and support for arts-infused lessons across the K–8 general curriculum. Finally, you read a number of wonderful "thumbnail sketches" of other lessons from our contributing teachers. The inclusion of their creative ideas was meant to inspire you to do more of the same.

In closing, throughout this book, you were guided through your own stages of planning by the inspiring stories of real teachers in real K–8 classrooms. They, too, embarked on a remarkable journey of curiosity, creativity, courage, planning, experimentation, reflection, and growth about arts-infused teaching across the curriculum.

Most of our contributing teachers began this journey with limited or no arts background. They, too, started with a belief that the arts may be important within their curriculum, yet they needed models of what forms that arts activity infusion might take. Now they have each successfully developed many original lessons and units where arts-infused teaching has indeed increased student participation, involvement, understanding, meaning making, and memory of the content learning at hand.

With these creative and courageous educators as our guides, may we all continue to find ways to deliver more arts to more students. For it is through these active and expressive avenues of learning that our students may become more wholly educated and humane.

References

McDonald, N., & Fisher, D. (2002). *Developing arts-loving readers: Top 10 questions teachers are asking about integrated arts education.* Lanham, MD: Rowan and Littlefield Education.

McDonald, N., & Fisher, D. (2006). *Teaching literacy through the arts.* New York: Guilford.

Resource Bibliography

Children's Literature about the Arts

Books about MUSIC and Musicians

Learning to Listen to Music

Deetlefs, R. (1999). *The song of six birds.* New York: Dutton Children's Books.

Ganeri, A. (1996) *The young person's guide to the orchestra: Benjamin Britten's composition on CD narrated by Ben Kingsley.* San Diego, CA: Harcourt Brace.

Gollub, M. (2000). *The jazz fly.* Santa Rosa, CA: Tortuga Press.

Levine, R. (2000). *Story of the orchestra: A child's introduction to the instruments, the music, the musicians and composers.* New York: Black Dog & Leventhal.

Krull, K. (2003). *M is for music.* San Diego, CA: Harcourt.

Kuskin, K. (1982). *The philharmonic gets dressed.* New York: HarperCollins.

Shaik, F. (1998). *The jazz of our street.* New York: Dial.

Weatherford, C. (2000). *The sound that jazz makes.* New York: Walter.

Lives and Works of Famous Composers

Celenza, A. (2000). *The farewell symphony.* Watertown, MA: Charlesbridge Publishing.

Downing, J. (1994). *Mozart tonight.* New York: Aladdin.

Fisher, L. (1996). *William Tell.* New York: Farrar, Straus and Giroux.

Gatti, A. (1997). *The magic flute.* San Francisco: Chronicle Books.

Isadora, R. (1994). *Firebird.* New York: Putnam.

Krull, K. (1993). *Lives of the musicians: Good times, bad times (and what the neighbors thought).* San Diego, CA: Harcourt Brace.

Pinkney, A. D. (1998). *Duke Ellington: The piano prince and his orchestra.* New York: Hyperion Books.

Press, D. (1994). *A multicultural portrait of America's music.* New York: Marshall Cavendish.

Price, L. (1990). *Aida.* San Diego, CA: Harcourt Brace.

Vernon, R. (1997). *Introducing Stravinsky.* Parsippany, NJ: Silver Burdett Press.

Vigna, G. (1999). *Masters of music: Jazz and its history.* New York: Barron's.

Books about Instruments, Singers, and Music Making

Ardley, N. (2000). *Eyewitness books: Music: Discover the world* of musical sound and the amazing variety of instruments *that create music.* New York: Dorling Kindersley.

Burleigh, R. (2001). *Lookin' for bird in the big city.* New York: Harcourt.

Clement, C. (1989). *The voice of the wood.* New York: Dial.

Curtis, G. (1998). *The bat boy & his violin.* New York: Simon and Schuster.

Cutler, J. (1999). *The cello of Mr. O.* New York: Dutton.

Dengler, M. (1999). *Fiddlin' Sam.* Flagstaff, AZ: Rising Moon.

Grifalconi, A. (1999). *Tiny's hat.* New York: HarperCollins.

Hopkinson, D. (1999). *A band of angels: A story inspired by the Jubilee Singers.* New York: Antheneum.

Isadora, R. (1979). *Ben's trumpet.* New York: Greenwillow.

Lacapa, M. (1990). *The flute player: An Apache folktale.* Flagstaff, AZ: Northland Publishing.

London, J. (1993). *Hip cat.* San Francisco: Chronicle Books.

McKee, D. (1991). *The sad story of Veronica who played the violin.* New York: Kane, Miller.

McPhail, D. (1999). *Mole music.* New York: Henry Holt.

Meyrich, C. (1989). *The musical life of Gustav Mole.* New York: Child's Play International.

Moss, L. (1995). *Zin! Zin! Zin! A violin.* New York: Simon and Schuster.

Rockwell, N. (1997). *Willie was different: A children's story by Norman Rockwell.* New York: Dragonfly Books by Alfred A. Knopf.

Schroeder, A. (1996). *Satchmo's blues.* New York: Doubleday.

Turner, B. (1996). *The living violin.* New York: Knopf.

Books with Song Texts

Birdseye, T., & Birdseye, G. (1994). *She'll be comin' round the mountain.* New York: Holiday House.

Catalano, D. (1998). *Frog went a-courting: A musical play in six acts.* Honesdale, PA: Boyds Mills Press.

Conrad, P. (1985). *Prairie songs.* New York: Harper-Collins.

Manson, C. (1993). *Over the river and through the wood.* New York: North-South Books.

Mattox, C. (1989). *Shake it to the one that you live the best: Play songs and lullabies from black musical traditions.* Nashville, TN: JTG.

McGill, A. (2000). *In the hallow of your hand: Slave lullabies.* Boston: Houghton Mifflin.

Milnes, G. (1990). *Granny will your dog bite and other mountain rhymes.* New York: Knopf.

Raschka, C. (1998). *Simple gifts.* New York: Holt.

Saport, L. (1999). *All the pretty little horses: A traditional lullaby.* New York: Clarion Books.

Spier, P. (1970). *The Erie Canal.* New York: Doubleday.

Taback, S. (1999). *Joseph had a little overcoat.* New York: Viking.

Weiss, G., & Thiele, B. (1967). *What a wonderful world.* Littleton, MA: Sundance.

Westcott, N. (1989). *Skip to my lou.* Boston: Little & Brown.

Winter, J. (1998). *Follow the drinking gourd.* New York: Knopf.

Yolen, J. (1992). *Street rhymes around the world.* Honesdale, PA: Boyds Mills Press.

Poetry and Rhythmic Text (Music and Movement)

Hopkins, L. (1997). *Song and dance.* New York: Simon and Schuster.
Igus, T. (1998). *I see the rhythm.* San Francisco: Children's Book Press.
Jabar, C. (1992). *Shimmy shake earthquake: Don't forget to dance poems.* Boston: Little, Brown.
Shields, C., & Junakovic, S. (2000). *Music.* New York: Handprint Books.

Books about VISUAL ART and Artists: Learning to Look at Art

Brown, R. (1982). *If at first you do not see.* New York: Henry Holt.
Carle, E. (1984). *The mixed-up chameleon.* New York: HarperCollins.
Carle, E. (1992). *Draw me a star.* New York: Philomel.
Collins, P. (1992). *I am an artist.* Brookfield, CN: Millbrook Press.
Lionni, L. (1995). *Matthew's dream.* New York: Knopf.
Metropolitan Museum of Art. (2005). *Museum shapes.* New York: Little, Brown.
Raczka, B. (2002). *No one saw: Ordinary things through the eyes of an artist.* Brookfield, CN: Millbrook Press.
Wolfe, G. (1999). *Oxford first book of art.* New York: Oxford University Press.

What Is Art? What Do Artists Do? Concepts, Elements, and Tools Artists Use

dePaola, T. (1989). *The art lesson.* New York: Putnam & Grosset.
Gibbons, G. (2000). *The art box.* New York: Holiday House.
Heller, R. (1995). *Color.* New York: Puffin Books.
Karas, G. (2001). *The class artist.* New York: Greenwillow.
Rylant, C. (1988). *All I see.* New York: Orchard Books.

Lives and Works of Great Painters

Degas:
Littlesugar, A. (1999). *Marie in fourth position: The story of Degas' "The Little Dancer."* New York: Paperstar.

Matisse:
Boutan, M. (1996). *Matisse: Art activity pack.* New York: Chronicle Books.
Johnson, K., & O'Connor, J. (2002). *Henri Matisse: Drawing with scissors.* New York: Gosset & Dunlap.
Le Tord, B. (1999). *A bird or two: A story about Henri Matisse.* Grand Rapids, MI: Eerdmans Books.
Welton, J. (2002). *Henri Matisse: Artists in their time.* New York: Franklin Watts.

Monet:

Armstrong, C. (1995). *My Monet art museum.* New York: Philomel.

Bjork, C. (1985). *Linnea in Monet's garden.* New York: R & S Books.

Boutan, M. (1995). *Monet: Art activity pack.* New York: Chronicle Books.

van Gogh:

Anholt, L. (1994). *Camille and the sunflowers: A story about Vincent van Gogh.* New York: Barrons.

Isom, J. (1997). *The first starry night.* Watertown, MA: Charlesbridge Publishing.

Waldman, N. (1999). *The starry night.* Honesdale, PA: Boyds Mills.

Additional artist study:

Ringgold, F., Feeman, L., & Roucher, N. (1996). *Talking to Faith Ringgold.* New York: Crown.

Sellier, M. (1996). *Chagall from A to Z.* New York: Bedrick Books.

Other artists featured in books by the same author and publisher are

Matisse from A to Z (1995) and *Bonnard from A to Z* (1997).

Stanley, D. (2000). *Michelangelo.* New York: HarperCollins.

Winter, J. (1998). *My name is Georgia.* San Diego, CA: Harcourt Brace.

Krull, K. (1995). *Lives of the artists: Masterpieces, messes, and what the neighbors thought.* San Diego, CA: Harcourt Brace.

Venezia, M. (1994–2001). *Getting to know the world's greatest artists* (series). New York: Children's Press.

The following painters are each featured within additional individual books in this series by Venezia: Frida Kahlo, Grant Wood, Andy Warhol, El Greco, Edward Hopper, Francisco Goya, Pieter Bruegel, Marc Chagall, Paul Klee, Henri De Toulouse-Lautrec, Paul Gauguin, Paul Cezanne, Henri Mattisse, Pierre Auguste Renoir, Monet, Picasso, Salvador Dali, Rockwell, el Greco, Diego Rivera, Michelangelo, Dorothea Lange, Mary Cassatt, Grant Wood, Rembrandt, O'Keeffe, van Gogh, Goya, Jackson Pollock, Alexander Calder, Da Vinci, Raphael, Botticelli, Degas.

Books about THEATRE

Bany-Winters, L. (1997). *On stage: Theatre games and activities for kids.* Chicago: Chicago Review Press.

Evans, C. (2008). *Acting and theatre.* West Chester, PA: Usborne.

Forward, T. (2005). *Shakespeare's Globe: An interactive pop-up theatre.* Cambridge, MA: Candlewick Press.

Glencoe McGraw-Hill. (2004). *Theatre: Art in action* (Student Edition). New York: Author.

Hal Leonard. (2004). *Music Theatre anthology for teens.* New York: Hal Leonard.

Lock, D. (2008). *A trip to the theatre.* New York: Dorling Kindersley.

Rubin, E. (1996). *Flip flap theatre.* LaVergne, TN: Ingram.

Schumacher, T., & Kurtti, J. (2007). *How does the show go on? An introduction to the theatre.* Burbank, CA: Disney.

Books About DANCE and Dancers

Allen, D. (2000). *Dancing in the wings.* New York: Dial Books for Young Readers.
Asher, S. (2001). *Stella's dancing days.* San Diego, CA: Harcourt Brace.
Cooper, E. (2001). *Dance.* New York: Greenwillow.
Glassman, B. (2001). *Mikail Baryshnikov: Dance genius.* New York: Blackbirch.
Glover, S., Weber, B., & Hines, G. (2000). *Savion—My life in tap.* New York: Morrow.
Martin, B., & Archambault, J. (1986). *Barn dance.* New York: Henry Holt.
McKissack, P. (1997). *Mirandy and brother wind.* New York: Dragonfly.
McMahon, P. (2000). *Dancing wheels.* Boston: Houghton Mifflin.
Pinkney, A. (1993). *Alvin Ailey.* New York: Hyperion.
Schroeder, A. (1989). *Ragtime Tumpie.* Boston: Little, Brown.
Walton, R., & Lopez-Escriva, A. (2001). *How can you dance?* New York: GP Putnam's Sons.

Resources for Teaching with the Arts

K–8 MUSIC Text Materials

National Music Series (K–8) (Grade-level music materials, CDs, DVDs, student and teacher's text editions, resource books, thematic indexes, etc.)

> NOTE: Check with your district and school site administrator and/or librarian for the name and location of your adopted basal series in music.

> *Making Music K–8* © 2005.
> Silver Burdett/Pearson Education
> Parsippany, NJ
> www.sbgmusic.com

> *Spotlight on Music K–8* © 2005
> Macmillian/McGraw-Hill
> New York, NY
> www.mhschool.com/products/music/index.html

Ancillary Music Text Series Materials for Classroom Teachers: Integrated Arts/Literacy Connections Across the Curriculum

> Making Music with the Arts and Across the Curriculum (Grades 1–6)* © 2008
> Silver Burdett Music/Pearson
> Parsippany, NJ
> www.sbgmusic.com
> *Available in selected states only

Materials for Teaching MUSIC Across the Curriculum

Anderson, W., & Lawrence, J. (1995). *Integrating music into the elementary classroom.* Belmont, CA: Wadsworth Publishing.

Ardley, N. (1991). *The science book of sound.* New York: Harcourt-Brace.

Ayensu, E., & Whitfield, P. (1981). *The rhythms of life.* Smithsonian Institute, New York: Crown Publishing.

Beall, P., & Nipp, S. (1994) *Wee-sing songbooks and CD's.* New York: Price Stern Sloan.

Blevins, W. (1999). *Phonemic awareness songs and rhymes.* New York: Scholastic.

Burz, H., & Marshall, K. (1999). *Performance-based curriculum for music and the visual arts: From knowing to showing.* Thousand Oaks, CA: Sage.

Fitzpatrick, J. (1997). *Phonemic awareness: Playing with sounds to strengthen beginning reading skills.* Cypress, CA: Creative Teaching Press.

Hansen, D., Bernstorf, E., & Stuber, G. (2004). *The music and literacy connection.* Reston, VA: MENC: The National Association for Music Education.

Kline, T. (1997). *Classic tunes and tales: Music listening lessons K–8.* West Nyack, NY: Parker.

Krull, K. (1993). *Lives of the musicians: Good times, bad times (and what the neighbors thought).* San Diego, CA: Harcourt-Brace.

Levene, D. (1993). *Music through children's literature: Theme and variations.* Englewood, CO: Teacher Ideas Press.

Marsalis, W. (1995). *Marsalis on music.* New York: W. W. Norton.

Marsalis, W. (2001). *Jazz for young people curriculum* [Recordings, teacher and student guides, video]. New York: Warner.

Scholastic Books. (1994). *Musical instruments.* New York: Author.

Materials for Teaching VISUAL ART Across the Curriculum

Arons, L. (1995). *Art projects made easy.* Englewood, CO: Teacher Ideas Press.

Backus, K., Evans, L., & Thompson, M. (2002). *25 terrific art projects based on favorite picture books (K–2): Easy how-to's for delightful art projects that enrich kids' reading experience.* New York: Scholastic.

Brittain, W. (1991). *Creativity: Art and the young child.* New York: Macmillan.

Chambers, J., & Hood, M. (1997). *Art for writing: Creative ideas to stimulate written activities.* Nashville, TN: Incentive Publications.

Chambers, J., Hood, M., & Peake, M. (1995). *A work of art: Creative activities inspired by famous artists.* Nashville, TN: Incentive Publications.

Cressy, J. (2001). *What can you do with a paper bag?* San Francisco: Chronicle Books, in association with Metropolitan Museum of Art.

Frohardt, D. (1999). *Teaching art with books kids love: Art elements, appreciation, and design with award-winning books.* Golden, CO: Fulcrum.

Henry, S. (1999). *Kids' art works: Creating with color, design, texture and more.* Charlotte, VT: Williamson.

Hierstein, J. (1995). *Art activities from award-winning picture books (PreK–3).* Carthage, IL: Teaching and Learning Company.

Hobbs, J., & Rush, J. (1997). *Teaching children art.* Upper Saddle River, NJ: Prentice Hall.

Johnson, P. (1997). *Pictures and words together: Children illustrating and writing their own books.* Portsmouth, NH: Heinemann.

Kohl, M., & Solga, K. (1996). *Discovering great artists: Hands-on art for children in the styles of the great masters.* Bellingham, WA: Bright Ring.

Krull, K. (1995). *Lives of the artists: Masterpieces, messes (and what the neighbors thought).* San Diego, CA: Harcourt Brace.

Massey, S., & Darst, D. (1992). *A complete history and appreciation program for grades K–8.* Upper Saddle River, NJ: Prentice Hall.

Ritter, D. (1991). *Literature-based art activities: Creative art projects inspired by 45 popular children's books: PreK–3.* Cypress, CA: Creative Teaching Press.

This K–8 text includes grade-level student and teacher editions, fine art transparencies, fine art prints, posters, unit resources, art history, integrated reading and writing workbooks, etc.

Schecter, D. (1997). *Science art: Projects and activities that teach science concepts and develop process skills.* New York: Scholastic.

Simpson, J., Delaney, J., Carroll, K., & Hamilton, C. *Creating meaning through art.* Columbus, OH: Merrill/Pearson Education.

Sterling, M. (1994). *Focus on artists.* Huntington Beach, CA: Teacher Created Materials.

Terzian, A. (1993). *The kids' multicultural art book: Art and craft experiences from around the world.* Charlotte, VT: Williamson

Turner, R., & Brooks, R., Clarke, J., & Chapman, S. (2005). *Art (K–8 basal visual art series).* Glenview, IL: Pearson Education.

Venezia, M. (1994–2001). *Getting to know the world's greatest artists.* New York: Children's Press.

This series includes separate books on the following artists: Frida Kahlo, Grant Wood, Andy Warhol, El Greco, Edward Hopper, Francisco Goya, Pieter Bruegel, Marc Chagall, Paul Klee, Henri De Toulouse-Lautrec, Paul Gauguin, Cezanne, Matisse, Renoir, Monet, Picasso, Salvador Dali, Rockwell, Diego Rivera, Michelangelo, Dorothea Lange, Mary Cassatt, Grant Wood, Rembrandt, O'Keeffe, van Gogh, Jackson Pollock, Alexander Calder, da Vinci, Raphael, Botticelli, and Degas.)

Materials for Teaching THEATRE Across the Curriculum

Baird, B. (1965). *The art of the puppet.* New York: Macmillan.

Balwin, P., & Fleming, K. (2003). *Teaching literacy through drama: Creative approaches.* London, UK and New York, NY: Routledge Falmer (Taylor and Francis Group).

Barchers, S. (1993). *Reader's theatre for beginning readers.* Englewood, CO: Teacher Ideas.

Bernardi, P. (1992). *Improvisation starters.* Cincinnati: Betterway Books.

Bony-Winters, L. (1997). *On stage: Theatre games and activities for kids.* Chicago: Chicago Review Press.

Bray, E. (1995). *Playbuilding: A guide for group creation of plays with young people.* Portsmouth, NH: Heinemann.

Caruso, S., & Kosoff, S. (1998). *The young actor's book of improvisation: Dramatic situations from Shakespeare to Spielberg* (Vol. 1). Portsmouth, NH: Heinemann.

Heinig, R. (1993). *Creative drama for the classroom teacher.* Upper Saddle River, NJ: Merrill Prentice Hall.

Kohl, M. (1999). *Making make-believe: Fun props, costumes and creative play ideas.* Beltsville, MD: Gryphon House.

Larrick, N. (1991). *Let's do a poem! Introducing poetry through listening, singing, chanting, impromptu choral reading, body movement, dance, and dramatization.* New York: Delacort Press.

Laughlin, M., & Latrobe, K. (1990). *Reader's theatre for children.* Englewood, CO: Teacher Ideas.

Lee, A. (1985). *A handbook of creative dance and drama.* Portsmouth, NH: Heinemann.

McCaslin, N. (1990). *Creative drama in the classroom* (5th ed.). New York: Longman.

Renfro, N., & Champlin, C. (1985). *Story telling with puppets.* Chicago: Chicago Press.

Rosenberg, H. (1987). *Creative drama and imagination: Transforming ideas into action.* New York: Rinehart & Winston.

Scholastic Education. (1993). *The world of theatre.* New York: Author.

Spolin, V. (1996). *Theater games for the classroom: A teacher's handbook.* Evanston, IL: Northwestern University Press.

Tarlow, E. (1998). *Teaching story elements with favorite books: Creative and engaging activities to explore character, plot, setting, and theme: Grades 1–3.* New York: Scholastic.

Wolf, A. (1993). *It's show time! Poetry from the page to the stage.* Ashville, NC: Poetry Alive!

Materials for Teaching DANCE
Across the Curriculum

Benzwie, T. (1987). *A moving experience: Dance for lovers of children and the child within.* Tucson, AZ: Zephyr Press.

Joyce, M. (1993). *First steps in teaching creative dance to children.* New York: McGraw-Hill.

Lloyd, M. (1998). *Adventures in creative movement activities: A guide for teaching* (2nd ed.). Peosta, IA: Eddie Bowers.

Longden, S., & Taucher, W. (2005). *Making music with movement and dance.* Parsippany, NJ: Pearson/Scott Foresman/Silver Burdett Music.

Murray, R. (1978). *Dance in elementary education.* New York: Harper's.

Rooyackers, P. (1998). *101 dance games for children: Fun and creativity with movement.* Alameda, CA: Hunter House.

Rooyackers, P. (2003). *101 more dance games for children: New fun and creativity with movement.* Alameda, CA: Hunter House.

Stinson, D. (1998). *Dance for young children: Finding the magic in movement.* Reston, VA: National Dance Association.

Arts Within and Across the K–8 General Curriculum (Books, Texts, Teacher Resource Materials)

Abrohms, A. (1992). *Literature-based math activities: An integrated approach.* New York: Scholastic Professional Books.

Arts Education Partnership. (2002). *Critical links: Learning in the arts and student academic and social development.* Washington, DC: Council of Chief State School Officers. (Entire publication available on-line at www.aep-arts.org/publications

Blecher, S., & Jaffee, K. (1998). *Weaving in the arts.* Portsmouth, NH: Heinemann.

Bloomfield, A. (2000). *Teaching integrated arts in the primary school: Dance, drama, music and the visual arts.* London: Fulton.

Brady, M. (1997). *Dancing hearts: Creative arts with books kids love.* Golden, CO: Fulcrum.

Burnaford, G., Arnold, A., & Weiss, C. (Eds.). (2001). *Renaissance in the classroom: Arts integration and meaningful learning.* Mahwah, NJ: Lawrence Erlbaum.

Burz, H., & Marshall, K. (1999). *Performance-based curriculum for music and the visual arts: From knowing to showing.* Thousand Oaks, CA: Corwin Press.

Campbell, D. (1983). *Introduction to the musical brain.* Wheaton, IL: Theosophical.

Cornett, C. (2006). *Creating meaning through literature and the arts: An integration resource for classroom teachers* (3rd ed.). Upper Saddle River, NJ: Prentice Hall.

This pivotal text includes multiple, highly comprehensive lists of resources, standards, lessons, teaching and assessment suggestions, and many model lessons and materials list for classroom teachers.

Dodge, D., Colker, L., & Heroman, C. (2002). *The creative curriculum: Connecting content, teaching and learning.* Washington, DC: Teaching Strategies.

Eisner, E. (2002). *The arts and the creation of mind.* New Haven, CT: Yale University Press.

Gelineau, P. (2004). *Integrating the arts across the elementary school curriculum.* Belmont CA: Wadsworth.

This important book includes information on theory, practice, and applications of arts standards, art forms, model lesson examples and many resources for classroom teachers.

Gust, J., & McChesney, J. (1995). *Learning about cultures: Literature, celebrations, games and art activities.* Carthage, IL: Teaching and Learning Company.

Jacobs, H. H. (1989). *Interdisciplinary curriculum: Design and implementation.* Alexandria, VA: Association for Supervision and Curriculum Development.

Jacobs, H. H. (1997). *Mapping the big picture: Integrating curriculum and assessment K–12.* Alexandria, VA: Association for Supervision and Curriculum Development.

Jensen, E. (2005). *Arts with the brain in mind* (2nd ed.). Alexandria, VA: Association for Supervision and Curriculum Development.

Hancock, M. (2007). *A celebration of literature and response: Children, books, and teachers in K–8 classrooms* (2nd ed.). Upper Saddle River, NJ: Prentice Hall.

This comprehensive text includes extensive resource lists of children's literature and literacy materials; thematic, literature-based, integrated teaching ideas and lesson plans; and model lessons featuring arts-infusion in reader response activities to literature.

Katz, S., & Thomas, J. (1992). *Teaching creativity by the working word: Language, music and movement.* Upper Saddle River, NJ: Prentice-Hall.

Kohl, M., & Potter, J. (1993). *Science arts: Discovering science through art expression.* Bellingham, WA: Bright Ring.

Levine, S., & Johnstone, L. (2000). *The science of sound and music.* New York: Sterling.

McDonald, N. (2008). Standards in the arts and arts within literacy instruction. In J. Flood, S. Brice-Heath, & D. Lapp (Eds.), *The handbook of research on teaching literacy through the communicative, performing, and visual arts, volume II.* Sponsored by the International Reading Association. Mahwah, NJ: Lawrence Erlbaum.

McDonald, N., & Fisher, D. (2002). *Developing arts-loving readers: Top 10 questions teachers are asking about integrated arts education.* Latham, MD: Rowman and Littlefield Education.

McDonald, N., & Fisher, D. (2006). *Teaching literacy through the arts: A guidebook for teachers.* New York: Guilford.

Piazza, C. (1999). *Multiple forms of literacy: Teaching literacy and the arts.* Upper Saddle River, NJ: Prentice Hall.

Prince, S. (2002). *Art matters: Strategies, ideas, and activities to strengthen learning across the curriculum.* Chicago: Zephyr Press.

Rabkin, N., & Redmond, R. (Eds.). (2004). *Putting the arts in the picture: Reframing education in the 21st century.* Chicago: Center for Arts Policy at Columbia College, Chicago.

Rothstein, E. (1995). *Emblems of mind: The inner life of music and mathematics.* New York: Times Books.

Selwyn, D. (1993). *Living history: Integrative arts activities for making social studies meaningful.* Tucson, AZ: Zephr Press.

Smith, S. (2001). *The power of the arts: Creative strategies for teaching exceptional learners.* Baltimore: Brookes.

Stake, R., Bresler, L., & Mabry, L. (1991). *Custom and cherishing: The arts in elementary schools.* Urbana: National Arts Education Research Center at the University of Illinois.

Williams, D. (1995). *Teaching mathematics through children's art.* Portsmouth, NH: Heinemann.

Resources for Integrated Arts Curriculum Planning and Community Resources Partnerships

Fineberg, C. (Ed.). (2002). *Planning an arts-centered school: A handbook.* New York: The Dana Foundation.

Remer, J. (1996). *Beyond enrichment: Building effective arts partnerships with schools and your community.* Washington, DC: American Council for the Arts.

Spenser, S., Wochowiak, S., Fisher, D., & Pumpian, I. (Eds.). (2005). *Challenging the classroom standard through Museum-Based Education.* New York: Lawrence Erlbaum.

Arts-Related WEBSITES, Contact Addresses, Catalogs

The Art Room
www.arts.ufl.edu/art/rt_room/

Arts Edge: Lesson plans and other resources provided by the Kennedy Center for the Arts
www.artsedge.kennedy-center.org

Arts Resource Connection: Arts education resource provided by Minnesota's Center for Arts Education
www.mcae.k12.mn.us/art_connection/art_connection.html

ArtsEdge: Many ideas for finding and using art in the general classroom
http://kennedycenter.org

ArtsEdNet: Extensive curriculum, lesson plans, and resources provided by the Getty Center
www.artsednet.getty.edu

Crayola Arts Education: Teachers and others share ideas, lessons, and arts advocacy
www.crayola.com

Culturefinder: The Internet Address for the Performing Arts: Large database of cultural events around the country, schedules and information, reviews, and news
www.culturefinder.mediapolis.com

eWorld: Learning Museum: Virtual tours of twenty-four art, history, and science museums
www.eworld.com/learning/museum.html

The Foundation Center: Provides guides to grant and research writing
www.fdcenter.org

GeoCities the Tropics: Lots of information on museums, arts styles and periods, and art education
www.geocities.com/thetropics/1009/index.html

Guggenheim Museum, 1071 Fifth Avenue, New York, NY 10128
www.guggenheim.org

Learning in Motion's Top Ten List
www.learn.motion.com/lim/links/linkman

Metropolitan Museum of Art, Fifth Ave. at 82nd Street, New York, NY 10028
www.metmuseum.org

Museum of Modern Art, 11 West 53rd Street, New York, NY 10019
www.moma.org

National Gallery of Art, 2000B South Club Drive, Landow, MD 20785
www.nga.gov

Music Educators National Conference (MENC): Many resources and materials for music education, including resources for classroom teachers (Music and Arts Integration)
www.MENC.org

On Broadway: Summaries of the season, many resources
www.artsnet. Heinz.cmu.edu/80/OnBroadway/

Storytelling, etc.
www.falcon.jmu.edu/~ramseyil/drama.htm

Virtual Museums
wwwmuseumlink.com

Visual Art and Writing
www.picturingwriting.org

World Wide Arts Resources: Over a thousand types of resources and links to websites.
http://www.wwar.com

World Wide Web Virtual Library: Includes a huge collection of art works that may be printed
out on a desk printer (Color clarity may not be the same as what is displayed online.)
www.icom.org

Arts-Related Catalogs/Websites for Materials and Teaching Resources

Educational Activities, Inc.
800-645-3739
www.edact.com

Films for Humanities and Sciences
800-257-5126
www.films.com

Kimbo Dept. J
800-631-2187
www.kimboed.com

MMB Music Inc. (General Music and Creative Arts Therapy)
314-531-9635

Rhythm Band, Inc.
800-784-9401

Suzuki (Music Supplies)
800-854-1594

Teacher's Video
800-262-8837
www.teachersvideo.com

West Music
800-397-9378
www.westmusic.com

Selected Journal Articles about Arts Integration and Interdisciplinary Contexts

Barrett, J. (2001). Interdisciplinary work and musical integrity. *Music Educators Journal, 87*(5), 27–31.

Barry, N. (1998). Arts integration in the elementary classroom: Conference development and evaluation. *Update: Applications of Research in Music Education 17*(1), 3–8.

Booth, D. (1985). Imaginary gardens with real toads? Reading and drama in education. *Theory Into Practice 24*, 193–198.

Busching, B. (1981). Readers theatre: An education for language and life. *Language Arts, 58*, 330–338.

Lamme, L. (1990). Exploring the world of music through picture books. *The Reading Teacher, 44*, 294–300.

Lapp, D., Fisher, D., & Flood, J. (1999a). Integrating the language arts and content areas: Effective research-based strategies. *The California Reader, 32*(4), 35–38.

Lapp, D., Flood, J., & Fisher, D. (1999b). Intermediality: How the use of multiple media enhances learning. *The Reading Teacher, 52*, 776–780.

Many, J., & Henderson, S. (2005). Developing a sense of audience: An examination of one school's instructional contexts. *Reading Horizons, 45*(4), 321–348.

Martinez, M. (1993, May). Motivating dramatic story reenactments. *Reading Teacher, 46*, 682–688.

McDonald, N. (2002). Developing arts loving readers: Creative response to music and art within children's literature. *The California Reader, 35*(2), 47–60.

McDonald, N. (2003). American panoramas: A literature-based integrated arts curriculum unit. *The California Reader 36*(3), 40–45.

McDonald, N. (2004). Haiku: Active learning with and through the arts. *The California Reader 38*(1), 18–23.

McDonald, N. (2005). Henri Matisse: Young reader's creative response to the artist and his works. *The California Reader, 38*(4), 14–21.

McDonald, N. (2006). Questions teachers are asking about literacy with the arts. *The California Reader 40*(1), 17–25.

McDonald, N., & Fisher, D. (2000). Tell them I sing: A dialogue on integrating curricula. *General Music Today, 14*(1), 13–18.

McDonald, N., & Fisher, D. (2002). Strings attached: A musical listening unit. *Music Educator's Journal, 88*(5), 32–38.

McDonald, N., Fisher, D., & Helzer, R. (2002). Jazz listening activities: Children's literature and authentic samples. *Music Educator's Journal, 89*(2), 43–57.

McDonald, N., & Fisher, D. (2004). Stormy weather: Leading purposeful curriculum integration with and through the arts. *Teaching Artist Journal, 2*(4), 240–248.

Snyder, S. (2001). Connection, correlation, and integration. *Music Educators Journal, 87*(5), 32–39.